"Hear, O Israel: The Lord our God, the Lord is one!"
(Deut.6:4NKJV)

The
ONENESS
of God

Rev. Dr. Caesar O. Benedo

The issue of the TRINITY has been an enigma in the Christendom long before the days of St. Francis of Assisi, afterwards and even up till today. The answers have not ceased to elude the church, as not all have reached a consensus. Jehovah Witnesses, the Jews and Muslims still disagree and the divide continues to deepen.

Christians insist that God is ONE but has many functions. So who is the Godhead? Who is Jesus? Who is the Holy Spirit? What are their roles? In this book, Benedo has provided the answers that prove that the Bible is not silent. The revelation he has received reinforces our belief that God's word is forever true and faultless.

If you have picked up this book that is because you are seeking the answer like each one of us. Now you have found the answers tell someone else.

- Jeanne-Frances N. Maduakor

Benedo's work "The Oneness of God" by the inspiration of the Holy Spirit who leads us into all truth is a must read for Bible Scholars and all who sincerely desire to be enlightened in the knowledge of God and Jesus Christ. Proverb 4:7 says, "… And in all your getting, get understanding."

- Rev. Egerton John-Otumu (D.D)

FOREWORD

The doctrine of the trinity – the teaching on the unity of God as subsisting in three distinct persons, is one of the teachings that is not fully understood and embraced by many in the Body of Christ. Till today, churches are divided on their stand on this very important subject. But as the days go by, knowledge is increasing and more light is being thrown on the subject.

In this book-'The Oneness of God,' Caesar Benedo presents a very deep insight into this subject and takes us a bit deeper in the understanding of the trinity of God. The exposition on different passages of the Bible that deal on the doctrine of trinity answers many long time questions, clears the ground of confusion and settles major controversies on the subject.

His approach on the different proposition involved in the subject is very insightful and informative. While this subject is purely a revealed doctrine, Benedo went a bit further by researching into issues around us that call us to reason, ponder and wonder at the wisdom of God in revealing himself to humanity.

Revelation is progressive. God has used Benedo to expand the boundary of understanding on this all-important subject. This will be a treasure in the library: private, public and Christian institutions and a resource material for anyone who wishes to do a further study on this subject.

-        Rev. Rotimi Oluwaseyitan

ACKNOWLEDGEMENT

A special thanks to the following people for their love, support and prayer to make this book a reality. Mr. and Mrs. Ononiwu, Mr. and Mrs. Ugwulor, Mrs. Sheyi Bonou, Pastor Fadel Akpiti, Mr. Samuel Fabrice Yomo, Pastor Samuel Kalu, Mr. and Mrs. Odjo, Mr. Kingsley Eme, Mr. and Mrs. Fajemirokun, Mrs. Vivian Asempapa, Mrs. Georgette Gbesset Baffoh, Pastor Veronica Bampoe-Darko, Rev. Emenike Paul Ezechiluo, Rev. Lucile Sossou, Prophet Holy Joy, Rev. Dr. Nicaise Laleye, Rev. Alphonse Dagnonnoueton, Rev. and Pastor Mrs. Tigo, Rev. Isidore Godonou, Rev. Mrs. and Bishop Meshack Okonkwo and so on.

A million thanks to the members of my family for your love, encouragement, care, and support. May God richly bless you all.

I want to use this opportunity to express my appreciation to Pastor Benjamin Opeyemi Olaosebikan, and Pastor Eric Osei Yaw for their brotherly support, encouragement, and prayer.

A special thanks to Bishop Kwesi Adutwum for your love, encouragement, advice, support, and prayer.

I'm indeed thankful to God for your life and for the incredible support you gave me. May God richly bless you.

I want to use this opportunity to express my gratitude to Pastor Zina Pierre for your love, support and prayer. May the Lord continue to bless you.

A special thanks to my Bishop, James Nana Ofori Attah for your love, encouragement, support and prayer. May the Lord continue to bless you.

A special thanks to Rev. Mrs. And Mr. Oluwaseyitan for the incredible support you gave me. Thank you for your love, encouragement, advice, and prayer. I admire your obedience to divine instruction and loyalty to spiritual authority.

I want to use this opportunity to express my gratitude to Apostle Michael Adeyemi Adefarasin for bringing out the best in me. I admire your commitment to excellence, your sincere desire to make a difference and your love for good work.

Words cannot convey how much I appreciate the love, care, support and prayer of senior deacon, and mama Georgina Lamptey for all the investment both of you made in my life. Thank you for standing by me at the very moment I needed it the most. May the Lord richly bless you.

DEDICATION

I dedicate this book to everyone who wishes to do a further study or broaden his or her understanding on the mystery of the Godhead, Christ, Holy Spirit and the church.

Table of Contents

PRAYER

Heavenly Father, in agreement with the Scripture that says the entrance of your word gives light and understanding to the simple (Ps.119:130), I beseech you to enlighten the eyes of my heart that I may understand the mystery of the Godhead, Christ, and the church as I read this book. Grant me insight and the grace to take hold of the truth, just as you did for Lydia in Acts16:14, when you opened her heart to receive the truth spoken by the apostle Paul about your Son Jesus.

By the power of the Holy Spirit, I pull down every imagination, argument and thought that does not conform to biblical truths, concepts and principles that the wicked may want to use to hinder me from accepting the truth in this book. It is written that I shall know the truth, and the truth will set me free (Jn.8:32).

Dear Lord, open my eyes to the truth in this book and deliver me from the spirit of error in Jesus name. Amen!

Listen, Israel: The Lord our God, the Lord is One. Love the Lord your God with all your heart, with all your soul, and with all your strength. These words that I am giving you today are to be in your heart. Repeat them to your children. Talk about them when you sit in your house and when you walk along the road, when you lie down and when you get up. Bind them as a sign on your hand and let them be a symbol on your forehead. Write them on the doorposts of your house and on your gates.

(Deut 6:4-9HCSB)

INTRODUCTION

D r. Wiersbe (a pastor, teacher, conference speaker and writer) explains in his commentary on Deuteronomy 6:4 that, "The Hebrew word translated "one" (ehad) can also mean "a unity" as well as "numerical oneness." It's used that way in Gen 2:24, describing the oneness of Adam and Eve, and also in Ex.26:6 and 11 to describe "unity" of the curtains in the tabernacle (see NIV)." [a]

He adds, "The word also carries the idea of "uniqueness." In contrast to the many pagan gods and goddesses, Jehovah is unique, for there is only one true God; He is God alone and not part of a pantheon; and He is a unity, which Christians interpret as leaving room for the Trinity (Matt 28:19-20; 3:16-17)." [b]

In response to the question, that one of the scribes asked the Lord Jesus about the most important commandment in Mark12:28, he answered him in verse 29 that the most important of all the commandments is "Hear, O Israel; the Lord our God, the Lord is one." Verse 32 informs us that the scribe agreed with Jesus' response as we notice in his words, "Well said, Teacher. You have spoken the truth, for there is one God, and there is no other but He." NKJV

The ONENESS of GOD

The Godhead is one true eternal God who created the heavens, and earth according to the Bible. He revealed himself in diverse way to humankind at different time in history because of his love and plan for humanity. However, the nature of his "oneness" remains a mystery to human race.

Colossians 2:9, declares that in Christ dwells the fullness of the Deity (some versions call this Godhead) in bodily form, while chapter 1:19 says God was pleased to have all his fullness dwell in him (that is, in Christ Jesus). Since the fullness of God refers to the sum of all that God is or the eternal constituents of his being, it stands to reason that the constituent elements of God wholly resides in Christ in bodily form.

Geoffrey W. Bromiley, (general editor of *International Standard Bible Encyclopedia* – revised edition), writes concerning the above passage, "The total expression "the whole fulness of the Godhead," then, signifies the sum of all that enters into the conception of "Godhead," God in nature, character, and being. All this dwells in Christ "bodily," i.e., in such a manner as to be shown in a bodily organism. [c]

The Bible affirms in John10:30 that Jesus and the Father are one. Chapter 14:10-11 reveals that Jesus is in the Father and the Father is in him. It adds that the words he speaks are not his own, but the Father who lives in him does the works, which means that the words and deeds of Jesus are the evidence of the Godhead dwelling in him. However, the manner wherein Jesus and the Father are one and how they mutually inhabit each other remains a mystery to the church.

INTRODUCTION

Although, a number of doctrines have been formulated since the beginning of church history to answer the many questions people ask about the nature and oneness of God, his Fatherhood, the person, Lordship, Kingship, Sonship and Deity of Jesus, the person and Deity of the Holy Spirit. A lot remains undone because of the wide spread confusion that exists about the concept.

The whole thing revolves around the Father, Son and Spirit being the different manner God chose to reveal himself to humanity according to Scripture. Some theologians employed the word "Trinity" to express the concept, claiming that God lives in three distinct persons. Others use "Oneness" to convey the same idea. To them, God is one indivisible being that manifests himself in three fundamental ways or roles to save humankind. Nonetheless, the subject has been a very controversial issue among Christians and non-Christian.

The Trinitarians believe there is one God that exists eternally as three distinct persons namely, God the Father, God the Son and God the Holy Spirit. To them, the three are co-equal and co-eternal. Many do not seem to agree with this concept because it entails tritheism, which is a belief in three gods asserting that the true God is one in being not three.

According to the Modalistic concept of the Trinity, "the Father, the Son, and the Spirit are not equally and eternally co-existent, but are merely three successive manifestations of God, or three temporary modes of His activity." [d]

The ONENESS of GOD

Oneness writer Rev. David Bernard says the Bible speaks of Father, Son and Holy Ghost as different manifestations, roles, modes, titles, attributes, functions of the one God not as three persons, personalities, wills, minds or Gods. [e]

Nelson's Bible Dictionary defines "trinity" as the coexistence of the Father, the Son, and the Holy Spirit in the unity of the Godhead (divine nature or essence). It adds, "The doctrine of the trinity means that within the being and activity of the one God there are three distinct persons: Father, Son, and Holy Spirit. Although the word trinity does not appear in the Bible, the "trinitarian formula" is mentioned in the Great Commission (Matt 28:19) and in the benediction of the apostle Paul's Second Epistle to the Corinthians (2 Cor 13:14)." [f]

Another time, in a discussion at the second-annual Elephant Room, which features what organizers call "conversations you never thought you'd hear" posted January 27, 2012 by Michael Foust-Baptist Press. Bishop T.D. Jakes says he has moved away from a "Oneness" view of the Godhead to embrace an orthodox definition of the Trinity and that some in the Oneness Pentecostal movement now consider him a heretic. [h]

I began to realize that there are some things that could be said about the Father that could not be said about the Son.

– T.D. Jakes [i]

INTRODUCTION

The reason modalism and tritheism came into being is that both stressed in an unbalanced way one aspect of the twofold truth of God's revelation in the Bible. Modalism takes one aspect of the truth – that there is only one unique God – and pushes it to a heretical extreme; tritheism, on the contrary, takes another aspect of the truth of God's revelation – that He is one-in-three – and pushes it to the opposite heretical extreme. [j]

As the church Fathers discussed the inner nature of the Trinity, they attempted to avoid the extreme of modalism on the one hand and the extreme of tritheism on the other. As they sought to formulate an adequate definition of the Trinity, they themselves were often accused of being either modalists or tritheists, depending upon their emphasis, at any given time, of one aspect of truth at the expense of the other. Their difficulty lay in trying to avoid sounding modalistic while speaking of the fact that we have one unique God, and to avoid sounding tritheistic while speaking of the three Persons and Their economy. [k]

The thought of writing a book on the subject came through the revelation God gave me concerning Christ and the church. My aim is to share the revelation knowledge and insight that I received about the mystery of the Godhead with others.

In 2003, I was in the house praying at about 11 p.m., when suddenly I heard one of the persons sleeping and snoring beside me calling my name and asking me to get closer. Initially, I did not understand what was going on until I heard my name about three times.

He said "Caesar, get closer, for I am the Lord your God. I have been seeking your attention, but you seem to be very busy with too many things, and this is why I have come to you this way — to show you deep and hidden things about Christ and the church."

When I heard that, I was a bit skeptical because I had never heard anyone say God appears to him or her in like manner. So I said to him, "If you are God, what is my mother's name?" I could have asked him some other question as a way of testing whether God was really the one speaking, but I believe the main reason I asked about my mother's name is that none of the people living with me in that house knew it.

We were about thirteen in number and I had not told any of them my mother's name because we all met at the place for the first time. Knowing also that God knows all things gave me the confidence to ask him something I knew the person didn't know about me. I said to myself, if God is the one talking through the person, he should know my mom's name.

In response to my question, he chuckled and said, "O Caesar," and then he kept quiet for a while before saying my mother's name. In addition, he told me deep things about my life and family that surprised me. In the course of our discussion that lasted about six hours, he did so many things that were naturally impossible and gave me several signs to prove he was the one speaking to me.

INTRODUCTION

As one of the signs, he revealed a deep secret to me about the person he was speaking through and one other person, and asked me to tell them what he has told me. Very early in the morning I went and spoke to them about it for confirmation. As I was speaking, both of them trembled with fear and wondered how I knew about their individual top secrets before I told them how the Lord revealed them to me.

Another surprise came when the people started asking me questions about the experience. They said, "We heard you talking throughout the night but we couldn't understand what you were saying; neither did we hear the voice of the person you were speaking to. Can you tell us what happened to you last night?" It was a big surprise to me because the voice of the person he spoke through was as loud and clear as mine. I could not figure out why they heard me talking for about six hours and none of them understood what I was saying or heard the voice of the other person even though some of them were lying beside me in the living room. Even those in the bedroom could hear me because the doors were opened.

It was a three-bedroom apartment, the inner room was for the boss and the other two were for us. The girls shared one room while the other one was for the boys. Since we were about thirteen in the house, some laid in the bedroom while others slept in the living room where I was praying. Throughout the night, none used the bathroom as they normally do. That was something I couldn't understand, because people wake several times to use the bathroom, except that night.

The ONENESS of GOD

That night, the Lord showed me several things about my life. He also spoke deeply about things that relate to Christ and the church from the Scriptures with detailed explanation of each point. After that encounter and other subsequent revelation I received, the burden to write a book and share with others the revelation knowledge God gave me became so heavy that I started gathering materials and outlining key points to research and meditate.

In 2005, the right approach to adopt in tackling the subject of the Godhead became very clear as the desire and need to write a book grew stronger in me. I began researching and writing from that year in spite of the challenges facing me at that time. The joy of wanting to contribute to the effort made by some in the body of Christ to answer many long time questions; clears the ground of confusion and settles major controversies on the subject kept me going for seven years.

The Bible made it clear in 2Peter1:2-4 that God has given us everything that pertains to life and godliness in proportion to the measure of the knowledge we have about him. In addition, we can possess his promises and participate in his divine nature by the same knowledge in order to escape the corruption that is in the world. Failure to obtain this revelation knowledge could result in spiritual frustration and death because people perish for lack of knowledge (Hosea4:6).

This book is designed to enlighten the body of Christ with revelation knowledge of the word of God about the true nature of the Godhead, who makes his light to shine in our heart to display the glory of Christ.

INTRODUCTION

The apostle Paul made an important declaration in 2Corinthians4:3-4, that if the truth of the gospel is veiled, it is hidden to those whose mind the wicked have blinded so that they cannot see the light of the gospel of the glory of Christ, who is the image and exact representation of the invisible God.

If the opinions of people about the nature of God, his fatherhood, person, lordship, sonship and deity of Jesus, person and deity of the Holy Spirit were to be sampled among believers, the result would be quite shocking as to the kind of responses they will give. In fact, some strongly affirm that the eternal God is one and only, he has no Son or any that is equal to him, Jesus Christ is merely a created spirit being like angels, higher than man is, but less than God is and holds an important position in heaven because he is the spokesperson of God. Adding that this is the very reason Scripture refers to him as the word of God. They also assert that the Holy Spirit is merely the active force or ability of God rather than a deity. Still others believe and confess at least one of the following (copied from different sources):

1. There are three persons in one God – God the Father, Jesus the Son and the Holy Spirit

2. There are three Gods in one person – God the Father, God the Son and God the Holy Spirit

3. God is one divine being taking on the different role of Father – in creation, Son – in redemption and Spirit – in regeneration like an actor changing scripts in film

4. God is similar to one egg with three parts (white, yolk and shell) or like H2O that can be water, steam or ice though each has unique characteristic and function, they all have sameness

5. God the Father became a Son through incarnation and a Spirit by virtue of his resurrection

6. Jesus had two nature namely: the divine nature wherein he is fully God (the Father) and the human nature by which he is fully man (the flesh)

7. That the divine nature (God the Father) left the body of Jesus at the cross so that the flesh he took for that operation can die for humanity since God himself cannot die

8. Any plurality associated with God is only that of attributes, titles, roles, manifestations, modes of activity or relationships to humankind

9. The "Father" refers to Jesus as God (spirit) while the "Son" refers to him as human (flesh)

10. God the Father became human in Jesus and after resurrection, he got a glorified, immortal human body and ascended to heaven

11. Jesus was the Father prior to incarnation and he became a Son only when he was made flesh

12. The Father, Son and Spirit are of the same substance and are co-eternal

13. The Holy Spirit is not merely an active force but a divine person

14. The Father, Son and Holy Spirit are essential parts of one being, just as man is made up of body, soul, and spirit

INTRODUCTION

15. The Father is the only person who is divine; the Son was created by the Father and the Holy Spirit was created by the Son

16. God is a universal mind, conscience, love, goodness and power filling all space and matter

17. Some consider the subject as something that transcends human knowledge, understanding and imagination

This book comes to add to the hard work and efforts of those who the Holy Spirit has used to enlighten the body of Christ on the subject and expand the boundary of understanding on the mystery of Christ and the church.

Finally, I cordially invite you to please join me and let us explore together, this vital and interesting subject: "The Oneness of God." As you read, be expectant and let the Holy Spirit use this book to illuminate your heart and transform you into the very nature of Christ's perfect image, by faith and revelation knowledge of God's word.

FOR DISCUSSION

Why do the Modalists claim that the Father, Son, and Spirit are merely three ways or modes of activity under which God manifests himself to humanity?

Why do the Tritheists believe there is only one true God that exists simultaneously as three distinct co-equal and co-eternal persons namely, God the Father, God the Son and God the Holy Spirit? Are there three Gods?

Did the Godhead first appears as the Father, latter as the Son and lastly as the Holy Spirit?

How do we avoid the heretical extreme of both modalism and tritheism?

The Bible says in 1Corinthians 15:24 that the end will come, when Christ hands over the kingdom to God the Father after he has destroyed all dominion, authority and power.

1. Who is the Father that Christ will hand over the kingdom to?

2. Will the handing over of the kingdom end Christ's reign?

3. What will become of Christ when the Father takes over the kingdom from him?

If Jesus were the Godhead, why would he make the following declaration? "In your own Law it is written that the testimony of two men is valid. I am one who testifies for myself; my other witness is the Father, who sent me." (John 8:17-18). If the body is Jesus, and the Spirit is the Christ as some claim, who is the Father that sent him.

Is Christ different from the Godhead and the Holy Spirit? If yes, how many God do we have?

Acts3:15, 4:10, 5:30, 10:40 and Ephesians1:20 declare that God raised Christ from the dead on the third day and sat him at his right hand in the heavenly realm.

1. Where is the God who raised Christ from the dead?

2. Who is he?

3. How did he do it?

Did Christ exist prior to the incarnation of God's Word? If yes, how did he pre-exist?

Is Jesus of Nazareth the Son of God or God the Son? What differentiate the first from the latter?

Did God the Father take on human flesh in Jesus at a precise moment in time, while remaining fully and eternally God?

Is Christ the Father that came into union with human nature to form the Son of God? Is Christ different from Jesus? If yes, what is the difference?

Why does the Scripture present Christ as both the Son of God and the Son of Man?

FOR DISCUSSION

Is Christ called the Word of God simply because he faithfully declared God's word?

Is Christ the Father that came into union with human nature to form the Son of God? Is Christ different from Jesus? If yes, what is the difference?

Why does the Scripture present Christ as both the Son of God and the Son of Man?

Is Christ called the Word of God simply because he faithfully declared God's word?

Can God die? If no, why was it possible for Jesus to die?

Ephesians 1:20 affirms God raised Christ from the dead and sat him at his right hand in the heavenly realm while Acts2:34-35 says, "The Lord said unto my Lord; sit at my right hand until I make your enemies a footstool for your feet." How many thrones are there in heaven?

Mark 16:19 declares Jesus ascended to heaven and sat at the right hand of God, while Acts7:55-56 says Stephen saw him standing at the right hand of God. Is Jesus sitting or standing in heaven?

Why was it important for Mary to play a role in the incarnation of God's Word?

Why couldn't God caused his Word to jump out of eternity to time by his great power?

Why was it necessary for God to prepare a body for Christ (Heb.10:5)?

The ONENESS of GOD

Why is Christ referred to as the possessor of the seven-fold Spirit of God (Rev.3:1)?

Why is the Holy Spirit called the Spirit of Christ (Rom.8:9) or the Spirit of the Son of God (Gal.4:6)?

The Prophet Daniel wrote in 7:13-14, "In my vision at night I looked, and there before me was one like a son of man, coming with the clouds of heaven. He approached the Ancient of Days and was led into his presence. He was given authority, glory and sovereign power; all peoples, nations and men of every language worshiped him. His dominion is an everlasting dominion that will not pass away, and his kingdom is one that will never be destroyed."

1. Who is the Son of Man?

2. Who is the Ancient of Days?

3. Where did the Son of Man come from?

4. Why did he approach the Ancient of Days?

5. Why was the Son of Man given authority, glory and sovereign power?

6. Why will his dominion and kingdom last forever?

7. Why must people from all nations worship him?

Is it appropriate to use words like "Oneness," "Trinity" or "Person" to express the truth revealed in the Bible about the nature of God or hold strictly to biblical terminology?

Why did Jesus use words that were familiar with the people of his time to explain the secret of the kingdom of heaven?

FOR DISCUSSION

When we get to heaven, are we going to see one person sitting on the throne as God or three distinct persons sitting on three thrones?

Why is God referred to as the head of Christ (1Co.11:3)?

Does God really want humans to have true understanding of the nature of his being?

Can our finite mind comprehend the things of an infinite God?

Is the Bible confusing? If yes, is God the author of confusion?

CHAPTER 1

NATURE OF GOD

STUDY QUESTIONS

1. Who is God?

2. What are the constituents of his being?

3. What is the central truth about his deity?

4. What are the attributes of his divine nature?

5. How does he reveal his invisible qualities?

6. What distinguishes him from other gods?

7. Why do people sometimes take him for a mere force?

The Godhead is an invisible eternal self-existent, independent, all-powerful transcendent God from whom all things derive their existence whether visible or invisible. The Bible declares in Psalms 90:2 that before the mountains were brought forth, and before the earth and the world were formed; he is God, which means he exists before all things began.

The ONENESS of GOD

In his notes, Albert Barnes writes concerning this passage, "The idea is, that he was always, and ever will be, God: the God; the true God; the only God; the unchangeable God. At any period in the past, during the existence of the earth, or the heavens, or before either was formed, he existed, with all the attributes essential to Deity; at any period in the future-during the existence of the earth and the heavens, or beyond-far as the mind can reach into the future, and even beyond that-he will still exist unchanged, with all the attributes of Deity. The creation of the universe made no change in him; its destruction would not vary the mode of his existence, or make him in any respect a different being." [a]

In the same vein, Matthew Henry stresses that God's existence has no beginning or end. He writes, "From everlasting to everlasting thou art God, an eternal God, whose existence has neither its commencement nor its period with time, nor is measured by the successions and revolutions of it, but who art the same yesterday, to-day, and for ever, without beginning of days, or end of life, or change of time." [b]

Bishop T.D Jakes emphatically points out in his message entitled "The Secret weapon of ministry," preached August 22, 1998 that, "When it comes to God, he cannot be explained or proven." He adds, "He must be revealed … If God can be explained, then he is subject to intellect."

NATURE OF GOD

The Bible declares in Isaiah 44:6 and 24 that God is the Alpha and the Omega, the beginning and end, the personal creator and lord of all things, while Psalms 145:13 says his reign and dominion is from eternity to eternity.

You alone are the Lord; You have made heaven, the heaven of heavens, with all their host, the earth and everything on it, The seas and all that is in them, And You preserve them all. The host of heaven worships You.
(Neh. 9:6 NKJV)

Happy is the one whose help is the God of Jacob, whose hope is in the Lord his God, the Maker of heaven and earth, the sea and everything in them. He remains faithful forever.
(Ps.146:5-6 HCSB)

Understanding the nature of God is fundamental to Christianity because many false views and concepts that distort the truth revealed in the Bible about him are gaining ground, and leading people to error. Hebrew 1:3 says the Son is the radiance of God's glory and the exact representation of his being (some versions translate being as person), meaning that God is an individual being. Nevertheless, the true nature of his divine being remains a mystery.

Concise Oxford Dictionary – Tenth Edition includes in its definition of nature the following: the basic or inherent features, qualities or character of a person or thing, inborn or hereditary characteristics as an influence on or determinant of personality. That is to say, God's nature can be defined as the inherent characteristics, attributes or qualities that make him who he is. Since the beginning of church history, several attempts have been made to answer the various questions people ask about this subject because of its significant to the body of Christ.

The ONENESS of GOD

The *International Standard Bible Encyclopaedia* defines the Godhead as the Saxon equivalent of the Latin Divinity or Deity. It states that it is rendered concrete by prefixing the article to it. As "the Divinity," "the Deity," so also "the Godhead" is only another way of saying God, except that when we say "the Divinity," "the Deity," "the Godhead," we are saying "God" more abstractly and more qualitatively. That is, with more emphasis of the constitutive qualities which make God the kind of being we call "God." It adds, as manhood is that which makes a man a man, and childhood that which makes a child a child, so Godhead is that which makes God, God. [c]

Scripture says in John 4:24 that God is spirit, and Psalms 139:7-10 reveals there is no place any one could go and hide from his presence because he is everywhere at the same time. *The Free Online Dictionary* defines spiritual being as an incorporeal being believed to have powers to affect the course of human events. [d] Even though, the Godhead is spirit, he used several means from Genesis to Revelation, to reveal himself to humankind in words and deeds because of his love, purpose, and goodwill so that humans could know his ways, works, plans, desires and how to fellowship with him.

In spite of the different doctrines developed over the years to clear the ground of confusion on the nature of his being, people still hold diverse views and beliefs on the subject. Whenever some talk about the issue, it appears as if it cannot be truly understood.

NATURE OF GOD

Although, Psalms 145:3 made it clear that the mystery about the greatness of God cannot be fully understood by anyone, I sincerely believe we can have a true understanding of the subject by the help of the Holy Spirit.

Dr. Herbert Lockyer, Sr., (General Editor of *Nelson's Illustrated Bible Dictionary*) writes, "God may be described in terms of attributes. An attribute is an inherent characteristic of a person or being. While we cannot describe God in a comprehensive way, we can learn about Him by examining His attributes as revealed in the Bible." [e]

The Bible talks about the special grace God gave to the apostle Paul to understand deep mysteries about Christ and the kingdom of heaven. Paul was a man like none other because of the incredible encounter and experiences he had with the Lord. 1Corinthians 12:1-6 recounts how he (Paul) was caught up to paradise, where he heard inexpressible things, so deep that they cannot be expressed in words. Although, the Apostle could not tell whether it was in body or out of body experience, many theologians and Bible Scholars believe he was literally taken up to heaven by God and showed hidden things about the Godhead, Christ and the church.

So profound was Paul that the apostle Peter, who is reputed to be pillar among other apostles mentioned in his epistle that Paul's letters contain things that are hard to understand (2Pet.3:15-16).

The ONENESS of GOD

From the concept of grace to atonement, redemption, prayer, adoption, rapture, incarnation, faith, righteousness, curse, blessing, baptisms, sin, death, resurrection, judgment, giving and receiving, sowing and reaping, spiritual and governmental authority, regeneration, growth, maturity and so on, God made them known to us through his ministry.

In Romans1:20, he writes, "For ever since the world was created, people have seen the earth and sky. Through everything God made, they can clearly see his invisible qualities – his eternal power and divine nature. So they have no excuse for not knowing God." (NLT) Through the wisdom, grace and insight he received to understand the mysteries about the Godhead, he said the invisible attributes of God, which no human eyes can see have been clearly revealed to us. Moreover, we can understand it by the things God made, so that we are without excuses as to failure to discern and truly come to the understanding of the true nature of God's being.

In conclusion, he said this unseen attributes that make up the being we call God are his eternal power and divine nature. This means that the eternal constituent elements of God are his power and divine nature.

From the creation of the world His invisible attributes, that is, His eternal power and divine nature, have been clearly seen, being understood through what He has made. As a result, people are without excuse.

(Rom.1:20 HCSB)

NATURE OF GOD

That is to say, though God has many attributes like omnipresence, omnipotence, omniscience, immutability, rationality, intelligence, creativity, infinite, faithfulness, love, holiness, gentleness, righteousness, and more, his everlasting power, and divine nature are the two fundamental constituents of his being. This implies that every other known and unknown attribute of God be it natural or moral, absolute or relative, communicable or incommunicable, is a product of these two intrinsic qualities.

The word translated "power", which comes first in the order of things between the two constituents of God, is the Greek word "dunamis" and it matches the Strong's Number "G1411". According to Thayer's Greek Lexicon (Abridged), it means strength, ability or power. It adds, "Universally, inherent power, power residing in a thing by virtue of its nature, or which a person or thing exerts and puts forth." [f]

The word translated "divine nature," which comes second is the Greek word "theiotes" and it matches the Strong's Number "G2305." Thayer's Greek Lexicon (Abridged), defines it as divinity, divine nature.

According to the *International Standard Bible Encyclopedia* - revised edition, "The term theiótęs is an abstract noun closely related to tó theíon, derived from the same adjective, theíos. It is commonly understood as a summary term for the attributes of deity. However, the term merely "defines" with regard to essence, signifying "the quality of the divine," that character which makes God God, and sets Him apart as worthy of worship." [g]

The ONENESS of GOD

As a summary term for the intrinsic attributes of God, divine nature describes the core qualities that make God who he is, apart from his inherent force that resides in him due to his nature. The main composition attributes of God that this term sums up include the following: eternal, self-awareness, source, sovereignty, transcendence, righteousness, faithfulness, holiness, will and purpose, love, intelligence, infinite and so on.

Another similar term used by the apostle Paul is "Theotes" found in Colossians2:9. This speaks of the state of being God (Godhead) according to Thayer's definition. It matches the Strong's Number "G2320", and it means the totality or sum of all that makes God who he is, while the first only describes the key qualities or essence of being God, apart from his eternal power. Both the first and second terms only appear once in the King James Version of the Holy Bible.

From the apostle Paul's point of view, based on Romans1:20, the inherent eternal force that resides in God by virtue of his nature, which enables him to operates as he pleases, and the integral quality (essence) that makes him God are the two constituents of his being.

John Walvoord and Roy Zuck, (editors of the *Bible knowledge commentary*) mention that, "What may be known about God" (v. 19) is now called God's invisible qualities and identified as His eternal power and divine nature. Since "God is spirit" (John 4:24), all His qualities are invisible to physical eyes and can be understood by the human mind only as they are reflected in what has been made, that is, in God's creative work." [h]

NATURE OF GOD

God's attributes are spoken of by some as absolute, i.e., such as belong to his essence as Jehovah, Jah, etc.; and relative, i.e., such as are ascribed to him with relation to his creatures. Others distinguish them into communicable, i.e., those which can be imparted in degree to his creatures: goodness, holiness, wisdom, etc.; and incommunicable, which cannot be so imparted: independence, immutability, immensity, and eternity. They are by some also divided into natural attributes, eternity, immensity, etc.; and moral, holiness, goodness, etc [i]

The book of Deuteronomy reveals something about the nature of God in chapter 6:4, and it says, "Hear, O Israel: The LORD our God, the LORD is one." From this passage, we understand that the eternal creator and lord of heaven and earth is one eternal true God in essence. Dr. Lockyer, states that this revelation of God as one to the Israelites was a significant religious truth because the surrounding nations worshiped many Gods and had fallen into idolatry, worshiping the creation rather than the true Creator (Rom 1:18-25). [j]

Since Romans 1:20 establishes the fundamental constituents of God as his eternal power and divine nature, and Deutoronomy6:4 highlights oneness as the central truth about the nature of his being, we can say that though God is indivisibly one in essence, his being consists of his eternal power and divine nature. The Lord Jesus said in John 4:24 that God is spirit, and those who worship him must do it in spirit and in truth. God is an eternal Spirit, who deserve to be worshipped.

The ONENESS of GOD

As I mentioned earlier, when one of the teachers of the law asked Jesus the most important of the entire commandment in Mark12:28-29, he referred him to what was written in the book of their law. By saying, "The most important of the whole commandment is Hear O Israel, the Lord our God, the Lord is one." The Bible declares in Deuteronomy 19:15, Matthew18:16, and 1Corinthians13:1 that a matter is established by the words of two or three witnesses. In light of these three passages we establish the "oneness of God" as the central truth about the nature of his being, while his "eternal power and divine nature" as its constituents. That is to say, though God is one in essence, his being is made up of his eternal power, and divine nature. Unfortunately, many have taken him for a mere abstract concept or force that only transcends time rather than a living divine being.

The following Scriptures: Isaiah1:18, Romans9:19, 11:33-34, present him as a divine being with a mind, reasoning ability and will. He speaks, plans, loves, gets angry and interacts with his creatures. This means that God possesses all human traits and qualities such as emotion, desire, sensation, speech etc. (1Sam.15:10-11, 16, and 22. Is.14:24). God's eternal power that enables him to operate or function as he pleases without limit and his divine nature are what make up his being.

In summary, the Godhead is a spirit being, and he is indivisibly one in essence (Deut.6:4). His being comprises his eternal power and divine nature (Rom.1:20). He lives and reigns over all things forever.

Although we might not see him at all time, we can feel his presence and power in our lives at any moment because he reveals himself to whomever he chooses in presence, and power. In eternity past, his eternal power, and divine nature constitute the fullness of his being.

LESSONS

1. The Godhead is self-existent and transcendent.
2. He is all-powerful and self-sufficient.
3. He is the origin of all existing things.
4. He is indivisibly one in essence.
5. He lives and reigns over all things forever.
6. His invisible attributes are revealed through what he created.
7. He is one God whose being comprises his eternal power and divine nature.
8. He is not a mere force but a divine person because he possesses all the traits and qualities of a living being.

ETERNAL POWER OF GOD

STUDY QUESTIONS

1. What is God's eternal power all about?
2. How significant is the power to the Godhead?
3. What will the absence of this power mean to him?
4. How did it become the primary means through which God revealed the true nature of his being to humanity?

The eternal power of God simply has to do with the self-ability, strength, force, might or capability of the Godhead that enables him to do things, operates, and functions as God without hindrance. It is the inherent force that resides in him because of his nature.

His awesome deeds and dominion from eternity to eternity are attributed to his eternal power through which he brings all things under subjection to his own will and divine purpose.

Psalms 66:3 and 7 declare that the enemies of God submit to him because of the greatness of his power and that the reason he rules forever is due to his power. Prophet Isaiah also writes in chapter 40:26 that God brings out the starry host one by one calling each of them by name because of his great power, and incomparable strength. He adds, "Not a single one is missing."

God's eternal power comes first between the two constituent attributes of his being, which are his eternal power and divine nature according to Romans 1:20.

For ever since the world was created, people have seen the earth and sky. Through everything God made, they can clearly see his invisible qualities—his eternal power and divine nature. So they have no excuse for not knowing God.
(Rom.1:20NLT)

The eternal power of God is sometimes referred to in Scripture as the "mighty outstretched arm" of God that he used in bringing the children of Israel out of bondage when the Egyptians set taskmaster over them and refused to let they go out of their country to the land God promised their ancestors.

You saw with your own eyes the great trials, the miraculous signs and wonders, the mighty hand and outstretched arm, with which the LORD your God brought you out. The LORD your God will do the same to all the peoples you now fear.
(Deut.7: 19 NIV)

NATURE OF GOD

The Bible declares in Job 36:22 that God is highly exalted above all things because of the greatness of his power that enables him to do as he pleases with the forces of heaven and with the inhabitants of the earth, while Psalms147:5 says he is great and vast in power with an infinite understanding. Job 9:4 also mentions that he is profound in wisdom, immense in power and that no one ever resists him and comes out unharmed. This implies that his omnipotence, omnipresence and omniscience attributes are largely bound to his eternal power.

Glad songs of salvation are in the tents of the righteous: "The right hand of the LORD does valiantly, the right hand of the LORD exalts, the right hand of the LORD does valiantly!
(Ps.118:15-16 ESV)

Without the eternal power of God that exalts him above all things, he would be subject to time, space, and other factors that affect and limit his creatures. The uncountable mighty acts of God, the glorious splendor of his eternal kingdom, and his dominion that endure through all generations are due to the greatness of his power.

So that all men may know of your mighty acts and the glorious splendor of your kingdom. Your kingdom is an everlasting kingdom, and your dominion endures through all generations. The LORD is faithful to all his promises and loving toward all he has made.
(Ps.145:12-13 NIV)

The ONENESS of GOD

The outstretched arm of God that he used in performing miraculous signs, and wonders in Egypt became the primary means through which the nature of his being was revealed to humankind, because it distinguishes him from the gods of other nations. Since the world began, no other god apart from the God of Israel has ever gone to rescue his people from the hand of another powerful nation like Egypt. The God of Israel did it to show the world the greatness of his power. Psalms 106:8 says he saved them for the sake of his name, in order to make his mighty power known to all.

Yet he saved them for his name's sake, that he might make known his mighty power. He rebuked the Red Sea, and it became dry; and he led them through the deep as through a desert. So he saved them from the hand of the foe, and delivered them from the power of the enemy. And the waters covered their adversaries; not one of them was left. Then they believed his words; they sang his praise.
(Ps.106:8-12RSV)

LESSONS

1. God's eternal power is his self-ability that enables him to do things.

2. Without the power, God will be limited to time, and space like his creatures.

3. God's omnipotence, omnipresence and omniscience attributes are bound to his eternal power.

4. The eternal power of God comes first between the two constituents of his being.

5. God's eternal power is sometimes referred to as the outstretched arm of God.

6. God's eternal power is the primary means through which the nature of his being is revealed to humanity.

ETERNAL EXISTENCE OF GOD

STUDY QUESTIONS

1. When did God's life start?

2. Is God's existence merely unending?

3. What does it mean to refer to him as eternal?

4. What are the connotations of God's eternal existence?

To say that God is eternal, simply means he lives forever. In other words, his existence has no end. However, the Scripture affirms clearly that God's existence goes beyond endless life to that which has neither beginning nor end of days, because all things whether visible or invisible begin and end in him. God exists because he lives. He lives because he has life, which has no beginning or ending. To refer to God as "eternal Spirit" simply means the one who has neither beginning nor end of days, and this is what constitutes the very essence of his divine nature.

It is quite evident that the creator of all things first had life in himself before his creature could derive existence from him—he existed in eternity before creating the heavens, and the earth (Ps.90:2, Is.44:6).

The ONENESS of GOD

To affirm therefore that God is eternal goes beyond an unending duration of life to that which has no beginning or end because he is the source and origin of everything that exists. Revelation4:8 refers to him as the Lord God Almighty, who was – past, who is – present, and who is to come – future. The past, present and future are locked up in him, meaning that in essence, he is eternal – i.e. he is everything.

Apart from the points mentioned above, the eternal existence of the Godhead also has the following connotations:

1. FATHERHOOD: God is the source and origin from which everything derived their existence. He is the personal creator and lord of all things including the heaven, and the earth with all that is in them. Having created it all, he reigns, rules, sustains and preserves them by his eternal power that enables him to keep all things under control forever. Ephesians 4:6 says there is one God and father of all, who is over all, through all, and in all, while Romans 11:36 declares that from him, through him, and to him are all things.

2. ALPHA AND OMEGA: He is the First and the Last, the Beginning and End of all things because it all begins and ends in him. The Bible informs us in Revelation 21:6, that he is the Alpha and Omega, the First and Last, the Beginning and End because nothing exists outside him.

3. INFINITE: God is not limited to time and space for they are part of his creative activities (Gen.1:1-14). While he himself is spirit – he is everywhere at the same time working out his eternal purpose. He has no end and he cannot be measured or quantified – transcendent.

4. SOVEREIGNTY: He is the eternal Lord that reigns and rules over all things forever, and he does whatever pleases him with the powers of heaven and with the inhabitants of the earth to accomplish his desire and divine counsel from one generation to another. .Psalms 115:3 says our God is in the heavens doing whatever he pleases. The Bible also points out in Psalms135:6 that the Lord does whatever pleases him in heaven, on earth, in the sea, and beneath the earth. The Prophet Daniel writes in chapter 4:34 that God's dominion is eternal and that his kingdom endures from generation to generation. In verse 35, he says the Lord does as he pleases with the powers of heaven and the people of the earth so that none can hold back his hand or say to him "What have you done?"

In conclusion, God's divine nature being one of the two key constituent eternal qualities of his deity comprises his existence. He exists because he lives. He lives because of his eternal life, which has neither beginning nor ending. He is transcendence, sovereign, and he is the source of all existing things.

LESSONS

1. God has no beginning or end of days.

2. All things derived existence from him because he existed before them all.

3. To refer to God as eternal means the one who has neither beginning nor end of days.

4. God's eternal existence connotes fatherhood, infinity, sovereignty, beginning and end.

5. The past – yesterday, present – today, and the future – tomorrow are all locked up in him.

CHAPTER 2

NATURE OF GOD'S ETERNAL POWER

STUDY QUESTIONS

1. What are the constituents of God's eternal power?

2. How does God's creative power differ from his active power?

3. Why is the whole work of God attributed to his creative and active abilities?

God's eternal power being the inherent force that resides in him by virtue of his nature is one of the two key constituents of his being as I said earlier. The eternal power of God comes in two phases namely: The creative and the active power of God. The Bible says in Psalms 33:6 that God created the heavens and everything in them by his word and the breath of his mouth.

The Word and breath (Spirit) of God speak of his creative and active abilities (Gen.1:1-3). Although they differ in function, they are one in essence. The divine will and purposes of God are put to effect through his creative and active power, which means that all his mighty and awesome works in the beginning were accomplished through his creative and active abilities that constitute what is known as the eternal power of God.

CREATIVE POWER OF GOD

STUDY QUESTIONS

1. Is God's creative power a mere force or a living being?

2. What sacred name did God give him in the beginning?

3. How significant is the divine principle of naming things?

4. How does name reveal the true nature, state, mission and position of a thing?

5. Why did God ask Adam to name the birds and beasts he formed from the ground?

6. Why do many people misinterpret Col.1:15 and Pr.8:22 in the body of Christ?

7. Why does the Bible refer to the Word of God as the wisdom and power of God?

8. Why does Scripture say none of all that God created was made without the Word?

9. Why does Scripture say in the beginning was the Word, the Word was with God and the same Word was God (Jn.1:1-2)?

NATURE OF GOD'S ETERNAL POWER

As earlier mentioned, the creative power of God is one of the two components of God's eternal power. The name it is called from the beginning is the "Word of God." John1:1 affirms that in the beginning was the Word, and verse 2 says he was with God in the beginning (he exists prior to the beginning). Verse 3 declares that God made all his works through him, which means that everything visible or invisible came to existence through him (he acts). Verse 4 informs us that in him was life, and that the life was the light of all humankind (he lives). From this passage, we notice that the Word of God exists and acts. He exists because he lives, and he lives because he has life. He acts because he has the ability to do things. The existence and activities of the Word of God constitutes the two key elements that make up his being. Thus, he is not a mere spoken word since he lives and acts, which are the basic qualities of a living being.

In the beginning was the Word, and the Word was with God, and the Word was God. He was in the beginning with God. All things were made through him, and without him was not any thing made that was made. In him was life, and the life was the light of men. The light shines in the darkness, and the darkness has not overcome it.
(Jn.1:1-5 ESV)

Although some in the Christendom condemn the notion of separate persons or plurality of persons in the Godhead, Scripture cannot be broken. The Bible clearly reveals that the Word of God is not merely the spoken word of the Godhead but the sacred name given to his eternal creative power that had life and subsisted in him (the Godhead) as individual being in the beginning. In addition, Scripture declares him God because he is one in essence with the Godhead despite his individuality.

The ONENESS of GOD

The name "Word of God," was given to him because of the divine principle of naming things, which God established in the beginning as means of identification. The Scripture confirms this in Isaiah40:26 that God brings out the starry host one by one and calls every one of them by name. Psalms147:4, declares he counts the number of the stars and calls them all by name.

Lift your eyes and look to the heavens: Who created all these? He who brings out the starry host one by one, and calls them each by name. Because of his great power and mighty strength, not one of them is missing.

(Is. 40:26NIV)

He counts the number of the stars; He gives names to all of them. Our Lord is great, vast in power; His understanding is infinite.

(Ps 147:4-5HCSB

SIGNIFICANCE OF NAME

A thorough look at the Bible reveals that names have always played an important role from the beginning about revealing the true nature, state, mission and the position of a thing. When God created everything in the beginning, Scripture reveals that he gave them names according to the book of Genesis1:3-10. However, the living things such as the beast of the field and the birds of the air that he formed from the ground were brought to Adam to see what he would call them and whatever name Adam gave to each of the living creature remains its name till today (Gen.2:19-20).

NATURE OF GOD'S ETERNAL POWER

God used the event to teach Adam the role and significance of the divine principle of naming things as a means of identifying them. Second, God did not name the living creatures he formed from the ground because he excluded himself in the management and governance of earth affairs. Had he done it, he would have violated the principles he established when he said, "Let them have dominion ..." (Gen.1:26).

The only being that has legal authority to do things on earth according to Scripture is human (spirit with body). Dr. Myles Munroe says the human body keeps the spirit legal on earth. For no spirit can operate legally on earth without the cooperation, permission or invitation of a human being.

So the Lord God formed from the ground all the wild animals and all the birds of the sky. He brought them to the man to see what he would call them, and the man chose a name for each one. He gave names to all the livestock, all the birds of the sky, and all the wild animals. But still there was no helper just right for him.
(NLT)

Throughout Bible history, names have served as one of the primary means through which God's nature and his eternal power have been made known to humankind.

Baker's Evangelical Dictionary of Biblical Theology says, "God's "Name" is a summary statement of his own nature and of how he has revealed himself to the world; it becomes virtually synonymous with the word "God" itself." [a]

The ONENESS of GOD

In his book, *Understanding the purpose and power of prayer*, Dr. Myles writes that one of the Hebrew concepts for name is "the being" itself.

When the Godhead granted his eternal power the right to subsist in him as distinct beings (creative and active abilities), though with one essence, he gave his creative ability a sacred name called the "Word of God" as a means of identification. The name differentiated him from all other existing being that latter came into existence or that were rather created by the Godhead through him – the Word of God. Second, it also differentiated him from the other component of God's eternal power call the "Spirit of God" (active ability) that also subsists independently in God.

Then I saw heaven opened, and there was a white horse! Its rider is called Faithful and True, and in righteousness He judges and makes war His eyes were like a fiery flame, and on His head were many crowns. He had a name written that no one knows except Himself. He wore a robe stained with blood, and His name is called the Word of God. The armies that were in heaven followed Him on white horses, wearing pure white linen. From His mouth came a sharp sword, so that with it He might strike the nations. He will shepherd them with an iron scepter. He will also trample the winepress of the fierce anger of God, the Almighty. And on His robe and on His thigh He has a name written.
(Rev. 19:11-16 HCSB)

Then I turned to see the voice that spoke with me. And having turned I saw seven golden lampstands, and in the midst of the seven lampstands One like the Son of Man, clothed with a garment down to the feet and girded about the chest with a golden band.

NATURE OF GOD'S ETERNAL POWER

His head and hair were white like wool, as white as snow, and His eyes like a flame of fire; His feet were like fine brass, as if refined in a furnace, and His voice as the sound of many waters; He had in His right hand seven stars, out of His mouth went a sharp two-edged sword, and His countenance was like the sun shining in its strength. And when I saw Him, I fell at His feet as dead. But He laid His right hand on me, saying to me, "Do not be afraid; I am the First and the Last. I am He who lives, and was dead, and behold, I am alive forevermore. Amen. And I have the keys of Hades and of Death.
(Rev.1:12-18 NKJV)

From the above Scriptures, we discover that the "Word of God" is the name given to Jesus of Nazareth not only after his bodily ascension to heaven but from the beginning – i.e. before incarnation, for he was in the beginning with God like one that came into being with him (we shall prove this as we proceed). Therefore, to consider God's creative power, also known as the living Word of God as a mere force or power is a violation of biblical truth. In addition, it is a serious assault against his being as the self-existent Word of God. He had eternal life (in fact, Scripture refers to him as the eternal life that was with the Father – Jn.1:2), and he subsisted in the Godhead as a distinct being in role – divine creativity – in the beginning (John1:1-5). Some may object to this stating that the Word of God is nothing more than the thought and plan in God's mind since words are expressions of one's thought or imagination.

Rev. Bernard, stating the difference between the modalistic monarchians' concept of God and their definitions of the Logos and the Son from that of the Trinitarians writes, "Their basic position was that (the Logos in John1) is not a distinct personal being but is united with God in much the same way as a man and his word." In addition, he quoted Justin Martyr's description of the belief as follow, "It is a power 'indivisible and inseparable from the Father." [b]

The Trinitarians teach that the Word of God is a distinct being from the Godhead, while the Modalists believe the Word is God himself.

According to Rev. Bernard, the Greek usage of "logos" can mean, "The expression or plan as it exists in the mind of the proclaimer – as a play in the mind of a playwright – or it can mean the thought as uttered or otherwise physically expressed as a play that is enacted on stage." [c]

The Word of God is not merely a plan or thought that existed in the mind of God in the beginning. On the contrary, he is a divine being since Scripture declares him God (Jn.1:1). It is very easy to deviate from biblical truth when thinking about the nature of God especially when traditions, beliefs system and practices push us to interpret wrongly or bend biblical truths, concepts, and principles to justify our position, words and actions.

AGENT OF CREATION

The creative power of God was his agent of creation in the beginning (Jn.1:3). All things in heaven and on earth, visible or invisible, including spiritual powers, lords and authorities were created through him and for him. God made no single thing in all creation without him, and because he exists before all, they derived existence and have their proper place in union with him.

He is the image of the invisible God, the firstborn of all creation. For by him all things were created, in heaven and on earth, visible and invisible, whether thrones or dominions or rulers or authorities—all things were created through him and for him. And he is before all things, and in him all things hold together.

And he is the head of the body, the church. He is the beginning, the firstborn from the dead, that in everything he might be preeminent. For in him all the fullness of God was pleased to dwell, and through him to reconcile to himself all things, whether on earth or in heaven, making peace by the blood of his cross.
(Col 1:15-20 ESV)

WISDOM AND POWER OF GOD

The creative power of God is referred to as the wisdom and the power of God in Scripture (1Co.1:24). It is generally said that wisdom is the practical application of what you know. *Oxford Dictionaries* include in its definition of wisdom the following: the quality of having experience, knowledge, and good judgement, the quality of being wise. [d]

Encarta dictionaries also include in its definition of the word, the following: the ability to make sensible decisions and judgments based on personal knowledge and experience, (ii) good sense shown in a way of thinking, judgement, or action, (iii) accumulated knowledge of life or of a sphere of activity that has been gained through experience." [e] In a nutshell, we can say that wisdom is the practical application of knowledge.

According to the Encyclopedia Britannic, creativity means, "the ability to make or otherwise bring into existence something new, whether a new solution to a problem, a new method or device, or a new artistic object or form." [f]

In other words, creativity is the display of one's wisdom and ability. God's creative activities in the beginning were the display or demonstration of his divine wisdom and ability, which he brought to light through the things he made.

The Word of God being the creative power of the Godhead, the agent of creation, the wisdom and power of God and the one who subsisted in God in the beginning is the aspect of God that enables him to execute or logically put his divine knowledge to effect. This is so because wisdom means the right application of what we know – that is, knowledge.

With this in mind, it is logical to say the very reason Scripture affirms that not even one of all that God created was made without him [the Word of God], is because he is truly the wisdom and power of the Godhead that enabled him to put his expertise to effect in a logical way. God's creation activity was a display of his divine wisdom and power. You will all agree with me that it is one thing to know something and yet is another to put our knowledge to effect in a logical manner. Thus, the part of God's being that enables him to put his knowledge to effect in a logical manner is his creative power also known as the power and wisdom of God or the Word of God.

FIRSTBORN OF GOD

The creative power of God is referred to as the "firstborn of God." The Bible declares in Colossians 1:15-16 that he is the image of the invisible God, the firstborn over all creation and that by him, all things in heaven and earth were created.

NATURE OF GOD'S ETERNAL POWER

In addition, verse 17 reveals that he exists before all things and in him, they hold together. Hebrews 1:6 says when God brought his firstborn into the world, he said, "Let all God's angels worship him." Note here that Scripture did not say the "firstborn son" but rather the "firstborn," which in fact are two different things.

He is the image of the invisible God, the first-born of all creation; for in him all things were created, in heaven and on earth, visible and invisible, whether thrones or dominions or principalities or authorities - all things were created through him and for him. He is before all things, and in him all things hold together.
(Col 1:15-18RSV)

And again, when he brings the firstborn into the world, he says, "Let all God's angels worship him."
(Heb. 1:6ESV)

To refer to God's creative power as the "firstborn over all creation" simply denotes he was the first to obtain the right to exist as individual being before anything else came into existence. The Godhead granted his eternal power that is made up of his creative and active abilities, the legitimate right to subsist in him as distinct being because of his plan and purpose that he programmed before the world began to be put to effect by Christ – the incarnate Word of God – at the fullness of time. Jesus said in John 5:26 that as the Father has life, he also granted the Son to have life in himself.

For as the Father has life in himself, so he has granted the Son also to have life in himself
(Jn. 5:26RSV)

The ONENESS of GOD

In effect, the very first thing God did in the beginning was to structure himself in the light of his plans and purposes before engaging in any of his divine operations, which the Bible declare was realized through his Word. Titus1:1 and 2, talks about the faith of God's elect and the knowledge of the truth that leads to godliness, which is based on the hope of eternal life that God promised before the beginning of time. This reveals and confirms the fact that God planned his entire work before time began. To achieve all these, he allowed his eternal power to subsist in him as individual being and it subsisted as the Word and Spirit of God. John1:1-4 and 17:5 reveal that God's creative power is his Word that had life, glory and existed in the beginning as a distinct being.

In the beginning was the Word, and the Word was with God, and the Word was God. He was in the beginning with God. All things were made through him, and without him was not any thing made that was made. In him was life, and the life was the light of men. The light shines in the darkness, and the darkness has not overcome it.
(Jn.1:1-5ESV)

And now, Father, glorify me in your presence with the glory I had with you before the world began.
(Jn. 17:5 NIV)

Many in the body of Christ still misunderstand the portion of Scripture that refers to the Word of God as the "firstborn over all creation" (Col.1:15). To some, he was the first spirit created by God in the beginning before any other thing came to existence since Scripture declares in Proverb 8:22 that he was brought forth as the first of all God's work.

NATURE OF GOD'S ETERNAL POWER

They believe he was the only spirit being that God created directly before creating other things through him and that he holds a significant position and function in heaven because he is the spokesperson of the Godhead, hence, the name "word of God." Below is a quotation from "What Does the Bible Really Teach?" By Watch Tower Bible and Tract Society.

> ... As a spirit creature in heaven, Jesus had a special relationship with Jehovah. Jesus is Jehovah's most precious Son–and for good reason. He is called "the firstborn of all creation," for he was God's first creation (Colossians1:15) There is something else that makes this Son special. He is the "only-begotten Son." (John3:16) This means that Jesus is the only one directly created by God. Jesus is also the only one whom God used when He created all other things. (Colossians1:16) Then, too, Jesus is called "the Word." (John1:14) This tells us that he spoke for God, no doubt delivering messages and instructions to the Father's other sons, both spirit and human. Is the firstborn Son equal to God, as some believe? That is not what the Bible teaches ..., the Son was created. Obviously, then, he had a beginning, whereas Jehovah God has no beginning or end. The only-begotten Son never even considered trying to be equal to his Father. The Bible clearly teaches that the Father is greater than the Son. (John14:28, 1Corinthians11:3) Jehovah alone is "God Almighty." (Genesis17:1) Therefore, he has no equal. [9]

Still, others see him as one that existed with God in the beginning before any other thing came to existence. To them all things derived existence from him, which made him head over all creatures.

Dr. Wiersbe writes concerning this passage, "The term *firstborn* does not refer to time, but to place or status. Jesus Christ was not the first being created, since He Himself is the Creator of all things. *Firstborn* simply means "of first importance, of first rank." Solomon was certainly not born first of all of David's sons, yet he was named the firstborn (Ps 89:27). Firstborn of all Creation means "prior to all Creation." Jesus Christ is not a created being; He is eternal God." [h]

Similarly, *Adam Clarke,* in his commentary states, "If it is been said that God created him first, and that he, by a delegated power from God, created all things, this is most flatly contradicted by the apostle's reasoning in the 16th and 17th verses." [I]

In view of these different opinions, I would like to say that to be born or brought forth means to be engendered. If God's creative power is considered as his firstborn, it would logically mean he was the first to be brought to existence and caused to live by the Godhead before any other thing was created. How could one possibly make a being that already lives to come into existence, since he exists in God as part of his being in eternity past? To consider God's Word, as the *firstborn* has nothing to do with the Godhead creating him as some believe and boldly profess. Instead, it refers to the act of God granting him the right to subsist individually in him as the very first of his work that marked the beginning of his activities. Because he exists in God as one brought up with him in eternity past according to Scripture (Pro.8:23-36).

NATURE OF GOD'S ETERNAL POWER

I have been established from everlasting, From the beginning, before there was ever an earth. When there were no depths I was brought forth, When there were no fountains abounding with water. Before the mountains were settled, Before the hills, I was brought forth; While as yet He had not made the earth or the fields, Or the primal dust of the world. When He prepared the heavens, I was there, When He drew a circle on the face of the deep, When He established the clouds above, When He strengthened the fountains of the deep, When He assigned to the sea its limit, So that the waters would not transgress His command, When He marked out the foundations of the earth, Then I was beside Him as a master craftsman; And I was daily His delight, Rejoicing always before Him, Rejoicing in His inhabited world, And my delight was with the sons of men. "Now therefore, listen to me, my children,
(NKJV)

To say that God's Word is the firstborn of God simply denotes he was the first the Godhead granted the right to exist as distinct being. That is to say, the individual existence of God's creative power as the "Word" made him the firstborn over all creation. In a clearer way, we can say that God begot or engendered his creative power in eternity past from his eternal power, which is the first constituent of his being as his "Word" not as a "Son," and this act marked the beginning of his works. This occurred the moment God's eternal power obtained the right to subsist independently in God as the Word (creative ability) and Spirit (active ability) of God.

The ONENESS of GOD

The America Heritage Dictionary defines first-born as the "first in order of birth; born first." [i] This means that the very first thing God did in the order of his divine activities was to grant his eternal power the right to subsist distinctly as his creative and active power, and the name he gave his creative power was the "Word." This is why John1:1 says in the beginning was the Word, the Word was with God and the Word was God because the act of making him to subsist as individual being marked the beginning of God's works.

Proverb8:22-29 says God appointed him from eternity and gave birth to him (some versions use bring him forth) as the first of his works before his deeds of old. Some interprets this passage to mean "eternal generation or Sonship" but the problem with the concept is that it does not conform to the truth revealed in the Bible about the notion of divine Sonship (I'll expand on this as we proceed). For God to beget or give birth to him as the first of all his works refers to the act of making him to subsist individually from his eternal power as the "Word of God" rather than a "Son" because he became a Son at a specific time in history through incarnation. Whereas, what God did in eternity past that marked the beginning of his activities was to cause his creative power to subsist as a distinct being due to his eternal plans and purposes that he programmed to accomplish through Christ at a specific time.

God's eternal power, which is the first constituent of his being, becomes the source from where God's Word came forth and lived as individual being. This means that God did not speak his Word to existence as some affirm. On the contrary, he caused an aspect of his being to exist independently.

In summary, the beginning started when God's eternal power obtained the right for individual subsistence. Proverbs8:30 reveals that he was beside God as a master craftsman and that he was daily his delight, rejoicing always in his presence, while John1:1 tells us he was with God in the beginning and verse 3 asserts God made all things through him. That is to say, God allowed his eternal power to subsist as his "Word" and did all his works through him in a way that no single thing in all creation came to existence without him. Scripture beautifully says he holds all things together because he exists before them (Col.1:17).

JOHN1:1 AND 1JOHN1:2

For Scripture to say "in the beginning was the Word" highlights the fact that before time and all created existence began, he was present. Matthew Henry mentions here that the world was from the beginning, but the "Word" was in the beginning and that eternity is usually expressed by being before the foundation of the world. He adds, "The Word had a being before the world had a beginning. He that was in the beginning never began, and therefore was ever, *achronos* – without beginning of time."

Adam Clarke remarked,

*Before anything was formed-ere God began the great work of creation. This is the meaning of the word in Gen 1:1, to which the evangelist evidently alludes. This phrase fully proves, in the mouth of an inspired writer, that Jesus Christ was no part of the creation, as he existed when no part of that existed; and that consequently he is no creature, as all created nature was formed by him: for without him was nothing made that is made, John 1:3. [*k*]*

The ONENESS of GOD

Second, the "Word was with God" expresses the idea that he had a personal existence that distinguishes him from the Godhead just as a person is different from whomever he or she is with. Jamieson, Fausset and Brown, state in their commentary that it conveys two ideas namely: (1) He had a conscious personal existence distinct from God, as one is distinct from the person he is with, (2) He was associated with him in mutual fellowship.

According to John Walvoord and Roy Zuck, the word with translate the Greek pros, which here suggests in company with. [1] For the Word to be "in company with God" means he had a personal existence distinct from the Godhead.

The UBS New Testament Handbook Series provides further information on this passage that enhances better understanding of the text. It says:

The meaning of the preposition with (Greek pros) has occasioned some difficulty, but most commentators and translators apparently favor the meaning "to be with" or "to be in the company of." This preposition often conveys the sense of reciprocity, that is, the Word was not merely in the presence of God, but there existed a mutual and reciprocal relationship between the Word and God. This relationship must be expressed in some languages as "God and the Word were together." In other languages, however, an indication of purely spatial relation seems to be sufficient, and therefore one may say "the Word was there where God was" or "...in company with God." [m]

Third, the "Word was God," means that though he exists as individual being in the Godhead, he is not different from him in essence. He has eternal life, and constitutes an aspect of God's being known as the "creative power of God," which then made him equal with the Godhead even though he exists as a separate being. Marvin R. Vincent, (author of Vincent's New Testament Word Studies) explained here that, "The word "God," used attributively, maintains the personal distinction between God and the Word, but makes the unity of essence and nature to follow the distinction of person, and ascribes to the Word all the attributes of the divine essence." [n]

Fourth, that the eternal life, which was with the Father manifested and was seen, shows that though he was present with God in the beginning, he became flesh and dwells among us to save human race.

The Word became flesh and made his dwelling among us. We have seen his glory, the glory of the One and Only, who came from the Father, full of grace and truth.

(Jn.1:14NIV)

PLURALITY

OF PERSONS IN THE GODHEAD

The concept of plurality of persons in the Godhead is a biblical truth that some find very difficult to accept in the Christendom.

Oneness writer, Rev. Bernard rejects the view and strongly condemns it in his book "The Oneness of God," claiming that the "Word" is not a separate person from the Father any more than a man and his word are separate persons. To him, the Word is merely the thought or plan in the mind of God and the expression of God. [m]

From Scriptural point of view, plurality of persons in the Godhead does not indicate many or separate Gods in a united assembly as some think. Rather, it highlights the fact that though God is intrinsically one in essence, he allowed his eternal power being one of the two fundamental constituents of his being to subsist as distinct divine being, and it subsisted as his creative power – the Word of God and his active power – the Spirit of God.

The Bible declares in John1:18 that no one has ever seen God, but God the One and Only, who is at the Father's side, has made him known" (NIV). Another translation says, the "Only begotten Son, who is in the bosom of the Father" (NKJV). Still, few others use words like "the only begotten God" (NASB), "the One and Only Son" (HCSB), "the only God, who is at the Father's side" (ESV), "the only Son, who is on the breast of the Father, he has made clear what God is." (BBE).

David H. Stern, Ph.D. author of the *Jewish New Testament Commentary* asks, "What, then, does it mean to call the only and unique son "God," especially when the Son, who is God, has made him, the Father, who is also God, known? Is there more than one God?… throughout his Gospel Yochanan teaches that the Father is God, and the Son is God; yet he distinguishes between the Son and the Father, so that one cannot say that the Son is the Father." [n]

NATURE OF GOD'S ETERNAL POWER

In summary, God's creative power is one of the two components that make up his eternal power. He has eternal life, and he subsisted in the Godhead as individual being in the beginning. The "Word of God" is the name given to him from the beginning. God's works began from the moment he caused him to subsist independently. That is to say, the subsistence of God's eternal power as the "Word" and "Spirit" marked the beginning of God's activities, which Scripture affirmed was accomplished through him – the Word (Jn.1:1). He was in the beginning because it all began with him. Even though he subsisted as a distinct being in the Godhead, he is one in essence with him. For this reason, Scripture declares him God.

The creative power of God could also be referred to as:

1. The Word of God
2. The wisdom and power of God
3. The agent of creation
4. The firstborn of God

He [the Word of God] is one with the Godhead in essence not in person as some believe and teach. He is an extension of the Godhead, and the exact representation of his person to humankind so that whoever sees him sees the Father who sent him.

LESSONS

1. The creative power of God is not a mere abstract force but a divine being.
2. He is one of the two constituents of God's eternal power.
3. The *Word of God* is the sacred name given to him from the beginning.

4. The name serves as means of identification, which differentiate him from every other being.

5. The divine principle of naming things helps to distinguish one thing from another.

6. Names reveal the true nature, state, mission, and position of things because it defines them.

7. The Word of God is the agent of creation because God created all things through him.

8. He is the firstborn of God because he was the first to obtain the right for individual subsistence.

9. He is part of God's being not a created spirit as some claim.

10. He was present before time and all created things.

11. He is the part of God that enables him to put his divine expertise to effect in a logical way.

12. He is the wisdom and power of God, the Word, the agent of creation and the firstborn of God.

ACTIVE POWER OF GOD

STUDY QUESTIONS

1. Is God's active power a mere force or a living being?

2. What name is he called from the beginning?

3. Why was it necessary for God to give him a name?

4. What was his role in divine creation activities?

5. What role did he play in Jesus earthly ministry?

NATURE OF GOD'S ETERNAL POWER

Unlike God's creative power being the first component of his eternal power, the active power of God is the second constituent. He subsisted in the Godhead as individual being, though with one essence in the beginning just like the creative power of God, and the name he is called according to Scripture is the "Spirit of God."

And the earth was formless and void, and darkness was over the surface of the deep; and the Spirit of God was moving over the surface of the waters.
(Gen.1:2-3NASB)

It was necessary for the Godhead to give him a sacred name, just as he did for his creative power, because of the divine principle of naming things that he established as means of identification since both subsisted in him as individual beings. The name differentiated him from every other thing that latter came into existence. However, he is not a separate entity or deity in essence from the Godhead but an extension of his being, since he is one of the two constituents of God's eternal power that he granted the right to individual existence. That is to say, though he subsists separately in the Godhead, he is one in essence with him.

Oneness believers consider the above statement heresy because it indicates plurality of persons in the Godhead. According to their doctrine, the Father (Godhead) and the Holy Spirit are the same person because the term "Holy Spirit" is another name or title for God the Father. In his book "The Oneness of God," Rev. Bernard writes, "Father and Holy Ghost are simply two different descriptions of the one God." He Adds, "The two terms describe the same being but they emphasize or highlight different aspects, roles, or functions that He possesses." [a]

The ONENESS of GOD

Although, the Godhead and the Holy Spirit are one in essence, they are not in person. The Bible clearly reveals that the Father is an individual being different from the Holy Spirit even though they are one in essence. The Godhead is not the Holy Spirit neither is the Holy Spirit God the Father.

Although, the Godhead and the Holy Spirit are one in essence, they are not in person. The Bible clearly reveals that the Father is an individual being different from the Holy Spirit even though they are one in essence. The Godhead is not the Holy Spirit neither is the Holy Spirit God the Father.

But they rebelled, and grieved His Holy Spirit. So He became their enemy [and] fought against them. Then He remembered the days of the past, [the days] of Moses [and] his people. Where is He who brought them up out of the sea with the shepherds of His flock Where is He who put His Holy Spirit among the flock? He sent His glorious arm at Moses' right hand, divided the waters before them to obtain eternal fame for Himself, and led them through the depths like a horse in the wilderness, so that they did not stumble. Like cattle that go down into the valley the Spirit of the LORD gave them rest. You led Your people this way to make a glorious name for Yourself.
(Is.63:10-14 HCSB)

The active power of God is not merely an abstract force as some have mistakenly taken him to be. Neither is he a creature or angelic being as others think. He is a living being just like the creative power of God is, because he has eternal life and possesses the whole traits of a living being since he moves, speaks, wills, works, desires, gets angry, interacts etc.

NATURE OF GOD'S ETERNAL POWER

The Bible warns us in Ephesians4:30 not to grieve the Holy Spirit of God, by whom we are sealed for the day of redemption. Acts13:2 says he spoke to the disciples and ask them to separate Barnabas and Saul for the special work he assigned them. Verse 4 reveals he sent Barnabas and Saul out on mission.

In the local church at Antioch there were prophets and teachers: Barnabas, Simeon who was called Niger, Lucius the Cyrenian, Manaen, a close friend of Herod the tetrarch, and Saul. As they were ministering to the Lord and fasting, the Holy Spirit said, "Set apart for Me Barnabas and Saul for the work that I have called them to." Then, after they had fasted, prayed, and laid hands on them, they sent them off. Being sent out by the Holy Spirit, they came down to Seleucia, and from there they sailed to Cyprus.
(Acts13:1-4 HCSB)

And coming to us, he took Paul's belt and bound his own feet and hands and said, "Thus says the Holy Spirit, 'This is how the Jews at Jerusalem will bind the man who owns this belt and deliver him into the hands of the Gentiles.'"
(Acts21:11 ESV)

But when he, the Spirit of truth, comes, he will guide you into all truth. He will not speak on his own; he will speak only what he hears, and he will tell you what is yet to come. He will bring glory to me by taking from what is mine and making it known to you. All that belongs to the Father is mine. That is why I said the Spirit will take from what is mine and make it known to you.
(Jn.16:13-15 NIV)

The ONENESS of GOD

The active power of God was the first manifestation of the Deity on earth and he was directly involved in the creative activities of God. The "Word of God" joined with the "Spirit of God" in divine creation activities. Psalms 33:6 says that the heavens were made by the word of God and the starry hosts by the breath of his mouth. The combination of God's creative power (the Word) and his active power (the Spirit) constitute the eternal power of God, which is one of the two constituents of God.

> But Peter said, "Ananias, why has Satan filled your heart to lie to the Holy Spirit and keep back part of the price of the land for yourself? While it remained, was it not your own? And after it was sold, was it not in your own control? Why have you conceived this thing in your heart? You have not lied to men but to God."
> (Acts 5:3-4NKJV)

Adam Clarke remarks, "Every lie is told with the intention to deceive; and they wished to deceive the apostles, and, in effect, that Holy Spirit under whose influence they professed to act. Lying against the Holy Spirit is in the next verse said to be lying against God; therefore the Holy Spirit is GOD." [b]

Dr. Stern phrased it a bit differently and said, "The Holy Spirit is thus identified with God." [c] We observe here that apostle Peter equates the Holy Spirit to God. The reason for such assertion is that God [the Father], and the Holy Spirit are one in essence despite the fact they both exist individually.

NATURE OF GOD'S ETERNAL POWER

The word "God" here is evidently used in its plain and obvious sense as denoting the "supreme divinity," and the use of the word here shows that the Holy Spirit is "divine." The whole passage demonstrates, therefore, one of the important doctrines of the Christian religion, that the Holy Spirit is distinct from the Father and the Son, and yet is divine. [d]

The conception and birth of the Lord Jesus, including his entire earthly ministry were made possible by the help and operation of the Holy Spirit (active power of God) according to the written word of God.

This is how the birth of Jesus Christ came about: His mother Mary was pledged to be married to Joseph, but before they came together, she was found to be with child through the Holy Spirit. Because Joseph her husband was a righteous man and did not want to expose her to public disgrace, he had in mind to divorce her quietly. But after he had considered this, an angel of the Lord appeared to him in a dream and said, "Joseph son of David, do not be afraid to take Mary home as your wife, because what is conceived in her is from the Holy Spirit. She will give birth to a son, and you are to give him the name Jesus, because he will save his people from their sins.
(Matt.1:18-21NIV)

Without him, nothing of all that the Father accomplished through Jesus, the incarnate Word would have been possible. The Lord Jesus tells us in Matthew 12:28 that he drives out demons by the Spirit of God. John the Baptist equally said in John3:34 that God gave Jesus the Spirit without measure.

The ONENESS of GOD

But if it is by the Spirit of God that I cast out demons, then the kingdom of God has come upon you. Or how can one enter a strong man's house and plunder his goods, unless he first binds the strong man? Then indeed he may plunder his house. He who is not with me is against me, and he who does not gather with me scatters. Therefore I tell you, every sin and blasphemy will be forgiven men, but the blasphemy against the Spirit will not be forgiven. And whoever says a word against the Son of man will be forgiven; but whoever speaks against the Holy Spirit will not be forgiven, either in this age or in the age to come.
(Matt.12:28-32RSV)

He who comes from above is above all; he who is of the earth is earthly and speaks of the earth. He who comes from heaven is above all. And what He has seen and heard, that He testifies; and no one receives His testimony. He who has received His testimony has certified that God is true. For He whom God has sent speaks the words of God, for God does not give the Spirit by measure. The Father loves the Son, and has given all things into His hand. He who believes in the Son has everlasting life; and he who does not believe the Son shall not see life, but the wrath of God abides on him.
(Jn.3:31-36NKJV)

In summary, the Godhead granted his "Word" and "Spirit" the right to exist as individual beings in view of his eternal plans and purposes that he programmed before time began to be accomplished in Christ. Although, the three (God, his Word and Spirit) exist as individual beings from the beginning, they remain one in essence because they make up the one true God.

NATURE OF GOD'S ETERNAL POWER

In his book, *The E-Myth Revisited*, business consultant and author Michael E. Gerber explains a business idea that in my opinion, illustrates the notion of the Triune God. He points out that in everybody who goes into business there are three personalities: the entrepreneur, the manager and the technician (three-people-in-one). He describes the entrepreneur as the dreamer and visionary. The manager as the one who plans and maintains order, while the technicians is the doer or the one who executes the plans.

He writes, "An entrepreneurial business, without a Manager to give it order and without a Technician to put it to work, is doomed to suffer an early, and probably very dramatic, death. And that a Manager-driven business, without an Entrepreneur or a Technician to play their absolutely critical roles, will put things into little gray boxes over and over again, only to realize too late that there's no reason for the things or the boxes she put them into! Such a business will die very neatly." [e]

The plurality of persons in the Godhead does not signify separate gods or deities. On the contrary, it highlights the existence of the one God in three individual beings as the Godhead, his Word and Spirit.

LESSONS

1. The active power of God is not a mere abstract force but a divine being.
2. He is the second constituent of God's eternal power.

The ONENESS of GOD

3. He subsisted in the Godhead as individual being in the beginning.

4. The sacred name given to him in the beginning is the "Spirit of God."

5. The name serves as means of identification to differentiate him from other things.

6. He was the first manifestation of the Deity on earth.

7. He was directly involved in the creation activities of God in the beginning.

8. Without him, none of all that the Father accomplished through Jesus would have been possible.

CHAPTER 3

THE WORD MADE FLESH

STUDY QUESTIONS

1. Did God's Word really become flesh?

2. If yes, how did it happen?

3. Why was he incarnated?

4. Why do majority seem to be confused about the subject?

5. What is the significant of his incarnation to humankind?

6. Why is the incarnate Word call the Son of God?

7. How important is this subject to the body of Christ?

8. Why did the Holy Spirit come on Mary before the power of the Most High overshadowed her?

As I explained in chapter 2, the Word of God is a part of God that subsisted in him as individual person in the beginning (Jn.1:1). He is one with the Godhead in essence because he is an extension of his being. The Bible declares in John 1:14 that he became flesh and dwelt among us.

The ONENESS of GOD

The Word became flesh and made his dwelling among us. We have seen his glory, the glory of the One and only, who came from the Father, full of grace and truth.

(Jn.1:14NIV)

But when the fullness of time had come, God sent forth his Son, born of woman, born under the law, to redeem those who were under the law, so that we might receive adoption as sons.

(Gal.4:4-5ESV)

The incarnation occurred when the time fixed by the Godhead fully came according to the above passage of the written word of God. To do this, Scripture reveals that though he was in very nature God (that is to say, he is no different from the Godhead in essence even though he exists as separate being), he did not consider the equality with God as something to be retained. He stripped himself of all privileges, rights and dignity, took the very nature of a servant and became human in order to rescue humankind from sin, by offering himself on the cross of Calvary as sin offering.

Make your own attitude that of Christ Jesus, who, existing in the form of God, did not consider equality with God as something to be used for His own advantage. Instead He emptied Himself by assuming the form of a slave, taking on the likeness of men. And when He had come as a man in His external form, He humbled Himself by becoming obedient to the point of death—even to death on a cross. For this reason God also highly exalted Him and gave Him the name that is above every name, so that at the name of Jesus every knee should bow—of those who are in heaven and on earth and under the earth— and every tongue should confess that Jesus Christ is Lord, to the glory of God the Father.

THE WORD MADE FLESH

Rev. Bernard explains that the above passage means Jesus is God himself since it affirms he had the nature of God. Stating that God has no equal and that the only way Jesus can be equal with him is to be God himself. In conclusion, he said Jesus was equal with (the same as) God in the sense that he was God (the Father). [a]

As mentioned in previous chapter, Jesus is not equal with God because he is God the Father. On the contrary, he is one with God in essence because of his preexistence as the Word of God. Thus, verse 6 in the above passage tells us he exists in the form of God though; he did not consider the equality he has with him as something to be used for his own advantage. Had he done so, he would not have taking on the likeness of men. Verse 7 says he gave up the privileges, rights and dignity of being one with God in essence to be incarnated.

Although, Scripture states clearly that the Word of God truly became flesh and made his dwelling among humans. The mystery about his incarnation has remained a matter of incomprehensible facts that has not been truly explore nor understood by majority in the body of Christ. Whenever the question is raise among believers as to whether or not the Word of God truly became flesh, they will simply respond "yes" with scriptural attestation. But when it comes to the question of how he became flesh–incarnated, some seem to be confused or silent about it, while others merely quote the popular Scripture that says; "He was conceived by the Holy Spirit" from the gospel according to Matthew (Matt.1:20). At the end, we discover that many are without adequate knowledge and understanding of what they boldly profess.

The ONENESS of GOD

Now the birth of Jesus Christ took place in this way. When his mother Mary had been betrothed to Joseph, before they came together she was found to be with child of the Holy Spirit; and her husband Joseph, being a just man and unwilling to put her to shame, resolved to divorce her quietly. But as he considered this, behold, an angel of the Lord appeared to him in a dream, saying, "Joseph, son of David, do not fear to take Mary your wife, for that which is conceived in her is of the Holy Spirit; she will bear a son, and you shall call his name Jesus, for he will save his people from their sins." All this took place to fulfil what the Lord had spoken by the prophet: "Behold, a virgin shall conceive and bear a son, and his name shall be called Emmanuel" (which means, God with us).
(Matt.1:18-23RSV)

With this in mind, it becomes necessary that we seek to know and truly understand how God's Word became flesh and dwelt on earth. 1John 4:2 says every spirit that confesses that Jesus has come in the flesh is of God.

Beloved, do not believe every spirit, but test the spirits, whether they are of God; because many false prophets have gone out into the world. By this you know the Spirit of God: Every spirit that confesses that Jesus Christ has come in the flesh is of God, and every spirit that does not confess that Jesus Christ has come in the flesh is not of God. And this is the spirit of the Antichrist, which you have heard was coming, and is now already in the world.
(1 Jn.4:1-3NKJV)

HOW THE WORD BECAME FLESH

When God sent Angel Gabriel to a town in Galilee named Nazareth with a message to the Virgin Mary who was betrothed to Joseph (a descendant of King David), he said to her that she would conceive as a virgin and give birth to a son who she was to name Jesus. This message would have sounded abnormal because nature demands the union of a man and woman before conception could take place; and Mary was still a virgin to be married to Joseph. Confused, she asked the angel a very important and intelligent question on how a virgin could possibly conceive and give birth to a son without any union with a man.

The angel Gabriel explained in details how God's Word was going to become human in one verse of the Bible. This very passage becomes the central truth and primary key that would enable us to fully explore and understand the mystery about the incarnation of God's Word (Jesus of Nazareth, the Son of the living God).

The angel answered, "The Holy Spirit will come upon you, and the power of the Most High will overshadow you. So the holy one to be born will be called the Son of God."
(Lk.1:35NIV)

According to Rev. Bernard, this passage reveals that the Holy Spirit is the Father of Jesus Christ. "The one who causes conception to take place is the father. Since all verses of Scripture in reference to the conception or begetting of the Son of God speak of the Holy Ghost as the agent of conception, it is evident that the father of the human body is the Spirit." In conclusion, he said the Holy Ghost is the father of Jesus Christ, the Son of God. [b]

The ONENESS of GOD

In his book, *The most important person on earth*, Dr. Myles, writes, "In this passage is a fact of vital significance: the Spirit conceived God the Son or the King-Son, whose earthly name was Jesus, in the womb of Mary. Mary was what we might call a surrogate mother for the eternal and invisible God's entrance into the physical world as a human being." [c]

Joseph S. Exell, editor of *The Biblical Illustrator* comments on the passage as follow: "The way of the Spirit's powerful working to this miraculous conception is denoted by two words. One is, that the Holy Ghost should come upon her, not in an ordinary way, as in the conception of all men (Job10:8...)"; but in an extraordinary way, as on the prophets, and those that were raised to some extraordinary work.. The other is that the power of the Highest, which is infinite power, should overshadow her, to wit, make her, though a virgin, to conceive by virtue of the efficacy of infinite power, by which the world was created, when the same Spirit moved on the waters, cherished them, and framed the world." [d]

A closer look at the passage highlights three things that need to be considered. (i) The Holy Ghost will come upon you (ii) the power of the Most High will overshadow you (iii) the Holy one to be born will be called the Son of God.

HOLY GHOST
WILL COME UPON YOU

From the previous subject on the active power of God, we discover that the Holy Spirit is God's active power that enables him to do things. For him to come on Mary suggests God released his eternal self-ability on her, in order to empower her for the divine operation that was to take place in her womb – i.e. the supernatural or miraculous conception of his Word. Otherwise, it would be impossible for Mary to conceive

POWER OF THE MOST HIGH WILL
OVERSHADOW YOU

From our previous notes on the creative power of God, we also discover that the "Word of God" is the power and wisdom of the Most High according to 1Corinthians1:24. In addition, the Bible declares that God created all things through him (the Word). He is the creative power of God that subsisted in him (God) in the beginning (Jn.1:1-4). Thus, the power of the Highest, being God's creative power had to overshadow Mary who was already empowered by the Holy Spirit in order to be "incarnated" (made flesh).

HOLY ONE TO BE BORN

WILL BE CALLED THE SON OF GOD

The angel Gabriel states clearly that by reason of the Holy Spirit coming on the Virgin, and the power of the Highest being the Word of God, overshadowing her, she would supernaturally conceive a child who will be called the "Son of God," while Mary the mother would give him the name "Jesus" (Lk.1:31, 32). From this statement, we understand that God's Word was to be called the "Son of God" once incarnated. This implies that before then, he only exists as the "Word of God" rather than the "Son of God" because the rights of a son were to be confirmed on him after birth or through incarnation.

Interestingly, this same title "Son of God" given to God's incarnate Word was also given to the first man (Adam) who stood for the last (Jesus of Nazareth, the Son of God). Luke 3:38 says, "… Seth, which was the son of Adam, which was the son of God." the Bible also informs us in Romans 5:14 that Adam is a pattern of the one to come – that is, Christ.

And so it is written, the first man Adam was made a living soul; the last Adam was made a quickening spirit.
(1Co.15:45-KJV)

To understand the mystery about the incarnation of God's Word, we have to take a thorough look at the life of the first Adam, and see how he became a living being and dwelt on earth like the last – Jesus of Nazareth, since he was a pattern of the one to come.

FIRST AND LAST ADAM

STUDY QUESTIONS

1. What is the relationship between the first and the last Adam?

2. Why did God create a body for the first Adam to live in?

3. Did God also create a body for the second Adam?

4. How was the body of the last Adam prepared?

5. Why did God not cause him to jump out of eternity to time by his great power?

6. Why did the Virgin Mary play a vital role in the process of incarnating God's Word?

7. What is the basis for the humanity and divinity of God's Word?

8. What would have happened if he had stepped out of eternity to time without been born?

9. Why is Jesus of Nazareth an ideal man that differs from every other person on earth?

Then God said, "Let Us make man in Our image, according to Our likeness; let them have dominion over the fish of the sea, over the birds of the air, and over the cattle, over all the earth and over every creeping thing that creeps on the earth." So God created man in His own image; in the image of God He created him; male and female He created them. (Gen.1:26-27 NKJV)

In creation, the first man (Adam) was made in the image and likeness of God. He was a spirit being and he lived in the spirit world like his maker.

The ONENESS of GOD

Even though the original intent of his creator was for him to dwell on earth and manage all that was created, bear fruit, replenish the earth, multiply, subdue and have dominion over all things, he couldn't do any of that because it was impossible for a spirit to live on earth without a body. God had to form a body from the dust of the earth for him to live in (Gen.2:7). According to Dr. Myles, the human body keeps the spirit legal on earth. No spirit being has the legal right to operate on earth without the cooperation, invitation or permission of a human being. The reason is that when God created the earth, he gave it to humans and made it our domain (Gen.1:26). Psalms115:16, says the heavens belong to the Lord, but he has given the earth to humanity.

Then the Lord God formed the man from the dust of the ground. He breathed the breath of life into the man's nostrils, and the man became a living person.
(NLT)

If God has to come down from heaven to take dust from the earth that he used in making a body for the spirit-man of the first Adam to live in, it is reasonable to think the same for the last Adam (Jesus of Nazareth), because the first set a precedent for whatever follows. Moreover, when the last Adam came to the world, he said: "Sacrifice and offering you did not desire, but a body you have prepared for me."

... "Sacrifice and offering you did not desire, but a body you prepared for me; with burnt offerings and sin offerings you were not pleased. Then I said, 'Here I am — it is written about me in the scroll — I have come to do your will, O God.
(Heb. 10:5-7NIV)

Exell remarks, "It is one of the most striking things connected with our earthly existence that God sends no life into the world unclothed, bodiless. Every life has a body specially adapted for the service, which that life has to render. The higher the life the more complex the .organism; but in each case there is a wondrous harmony between every life and its embodiment and every body and its surroundings. If it be so, how much more when He will send His Son into the world will He prepare a body for Him – a body that shall be specially adapted for His great mission and for the accomplishment of His great design! The Incarnation is confessedly among the greatest of all mysteries." [e]

REASON
MARY PLAYED AN IMPORTANT ROLE

Before proceeding any further, let me ask a few questions that could pave way for better understanding of this subject. The Scripture plainly affirms that the Godhead is the Almighty with whom all things are possible for he can do anything at any time. Could he not have made his Word jump out of eternity to time? Since he is the all-powerful and self-sufficient God, who does whatever pleases him with the powers of heaven and with the inhabitants of the earth at any time or place, with or without human! Instead, he used the Virgin Mary to play a strategic role in the whole process of incarnating his Word. Could he have done this mainly because he needed a womb to incubate the incarnate Word? Or was it because he needed an egg or ovum from her that could be inseminated by his self-existent Word?

The ONENESS of GOD

I do not think there is any possible reason that anyone could put forward to justify the reason Mary appeared on the scene other than the simple fact she has an egg that could be inseminated by the living Word of God, through the operation of the Holy Spirit, and a womb to incubate the incarnate Word. In addition, she is the seed of Abraham, and a virgin from the lineage of King David.

Could we possibly think the eternal Lord and personal creator of heaven and earth had become weak that he could not cause the impossible to happen for his Word and make him step out of eternity to time? I sincerely believe the answer to all these questions is not far-fetched, because the principle established by the Lord in the beginning demands that every living thing whether human or animal coming to this planet must pass through the womb. That is to say, must be conceived and born in order to gain legitimacy as a living being, if not, the legitimacy of his existence on earth as human would be questioned; thereby bringing him under a curse for breaking the rule of nature.

About the framing of Christ's human nature in the womb of the Virgin, Exell comments: "The matter of His body was of the very flesh and blood of the virgin, otherwise He could not haw been the Son of David, of Abraham, and Adam, according to the flesh. Indeed God might have created His body out of nothing, or have formed it of the dust of the ground, as He did the body of Adam, our original progenitor: but had He been thus extraordinarily formed, and not propagated from Adam, though He had been a man like one of us, yet He would not have ban of kin to us; because it would not have been a nature derived from Adam, the common parent of us all.

THE WORD MADE FLESH

It was therefore requisite to an affinity with us, not only that He should have the same human nature, but that it should flow from the same principle, and be propagated to Him. And thus He is of the same nature that sinned, and so what He did and suffered may be imputed to us. Whereas, if He had been created as Adam was, it could not have been claimed in a legal and judicial way." [f]

Matthew and Luke showed that Joseph was a legal parent, but not a genetic parent to Jesus. Jesus was miraculously conceived in Mary, through the Holy Spirit. By virtue of being Mary's husband, Joseph was considered the father of Jesus. Since Jesus was born into Joseph's family, he was a legal heir. Through Joseph, Jesus obtained a rightful claim to the throne of David. Although Jesus was a legal descendant to Joseph, he was not a physical descendant. Luke's genealogy directly addressed this issue by stating Jesus was "supposedly the son of Joseph" (Luke 3:23). Clearly, people had assumed that Joseph was the biological father of Jesus, when in fact he was not (Matthew 13:55). [g]

With this in mind, it is logical to say the reason God brought in Mary to play a vital role in the process was that she had an egg (ovum), which contained half of the genetic material known as DNA needed for the development and formation of a living organism once inseminated. The insemination of this egg was going to constitute the basis for his humanity and a womb where the fertilized ovum incubated would be necessary for his development and growth. In addition, because she was the seed of Abraham whom God made the promise to and a virgin, which was one of the major criteria needed for the fulfillment of the prophecy, given by God in the Scripture concerning the incarnation of his Word.

The miracle of the virgin birth was not so much in the birth but, rather, in the supernatural conception of Jesus.

The ONENESS of GOD

There are five persons in Scripture with supernatural origins. Adam was created with neither male nor female parents. Eve's origin involved a man but no female. Isaac was born to parents both of whom were beyond the age in which they could physically produce children. John the Baptist was born to parents who were well into old age. But the greatest of the supernatural origins was that of Jesus, whose birth involved .a virgin but no man. [ʰ]

When gametes, which are the male and female reproductive cells, known as sperm and ovum fuse at fertilization, they form a diploid cell (zygote) with complete sets of chromosomes that gradually develop into an embryo. *The free online medical dictionary* defines fertilization as the union of male and female gametes to form the diploid zygote, leading to the development of a new individual. [I]

Chromosomes are thread-like structures located inside the nucleus of animal and plant cells. Each chromosome is made of protein and a single molecule of deoxyribonucleic acid (DNA). Passed from parents to offspring, DNA contains the specific instructions that make each type of living creature unique. [ʲ]

God's Word became flesh when he fused with an egg cell in Mary's womb, through the operation of the Holy Spirit to form a zygote with a complete set of genes encoded in the DNA (deoxyribonucleic acid). Some proof texts he preexisted and had life prior to his incarnation include the following: John6:33 (for the bread of God is he who comes down from heaven and gives life to the world), 6:38 (for I have come down from heaven not to do my will but to do the will of him who sent me). 6:51 (I am the living bread that came down from heaven.

THE WORD MADE FLESH

Whoever eats this bread will live forever. This is my flesh, which I will give for the life of the world), 6:62 (then what if you see the Son of man ascend to where he was before) and 17:5 (and now, Father, glorify me in your own presence with the glory that I had with you before the world existed).

Since he preexisted independently in the Godhead as his Word in the beginning, he was able to fertilize an egg in Mary's womb through the operation of the Holy Spirit, when he emanated from the Father to be incarnated.

Wikipedia, the free encyclopedia defines DNA as a nucleic acid that contains the genetic instructions used in the development and functioning of all known living organism. [k] The Bible mentions in John1:4 that the "Word" has life in himself. While 1John1:1 refers to him as the "Word of life" and verse 2 calls him the "eternal life" that was with the Father, which means the "Word of life" or the "eternal life" that was with the Father fused with the egg cell in Mary's womb.

A zygote is always synthesized from the union of two gametes, and constitutes the first stage in a unique organism's development. Zygotes are usually produced by a fertilization event between two haploid cells—an ovum (female gamete) and a sperm cell (male gamete)—which combine to form the single diploid cell. Such zygotes contain DNA derived from both the parents, and this provides all the genetic information necessary to form a new individual. [l]

The ONENESS of GOD

The zygote eventually developed into an embryo with half of its DNA derived from Mary, while the other half came from God's Word. This implies that a copy of his genetic makeup came from Mary (a human), and the other copy from the Word of God (a deity), through the operation of the Holy Spirit. As a result, the embryo inherited the characteristics of Mary and that of the Word of God or the eternal life that was with the Father, because its cell contains copies of the gene in her cell on which resides humanity and that of the Word of God in which resides divinity. The combination of these genetic materials constitute the basis for the humanity and divinity of the incarnate Word of God – Jesus of Nazareth, the Son of the living God.

A gene is the unit of heredity, which determines, or contributes to, one inherited feature of an organism (e.g. eye colour). Physically, a gene is composed of a defined DNA sequence, located at a specific place (locus) along the length of a chromosome and transmitted by a parent to its offspring. [ᵐ]

Hence, just as a male reproductive cell fuses with an egg at fertilization to form a diploid cell with the potential to develop into a new organism, God's Word inseminated an egg in the womb of the Virgin with his eternal life (1Jn.1:2, Jn.1:4). Humanly speaking, this is impossible but not with God. Jeremiah 32:27 says, "I am the Lord, the God of all mankind. Is anything too hard for me?" While Genesis 18:14 declares nothing is too difficult for God to do. For this reason, the Holy Spirit had to first descend on Mary to quicken her womb, select a seed- i.e. an egg to fertilize and cause the impossible to happen.

THE WORD MADE FLESH

The fusion of God's Word with the reproductive cell in the womb of Mary brought the "divinity" in the DNA of God's Word and the "humanity" in the DNA of Mary together to form a living being called Jesus of Nazareth. Consequently, Jesus was fully human and fully God while on earth because of his genetic makeup that was composed of both humanity and divinity. His dual nature blended so well that they are indivisible and inseparable. This is why he is both God and human in essence not in function, role or title.

Again, Rev. Bernard writes, "While the Bible is clear in emphasizing both the full deity and full humanity of Jesus, it does not describe in detail how these two natures are united in the one person of Jesus Christ. This, too, has been the subject of much speculation and debate. Perhaps there is room for divergent views on this issue since the Bible does not treat it directly." [n]

For this reason, many have ended up in error trying to figure out how divinity and humanity perfectly merged in Jesus. Unless his two natures are properly distinguished, there will always be fault with whatever doctrine we formulate on the subject. Some say the divine nature of Jesus is the Godhead (deity), while his human nature is the body. Others adhere to one of the following views: (copied from different sources)

1. Jesus was a spirit creature in heaven whose life Jehovah miraculously transferred into the womb of a Jewish virgin named Mary

2. The spirit in Jesus was God the Son who took on flesh to redeem humankind

3. Both the spirit and body of Jesus were created

4. Jesus was wholly human that was animated by the Spirit of God

5. Jesus became God from the moment he was baptized

6. Jesus was a human who became God when he rose from death

7. Jesus became God when he was exalted

8. Jesus was a demigod while on earth

In his book, *the most important person on earth,* under the heading "One with God," Dr. Myles writes, "… we talked about the fact that Jesus is fully God, even though he is also fully human. God the Son became Jesus of Nazareth for the purpose of his redemptive task in the world. His dual nature never diminished His oneness and equality with the Father." [o]

To Rev. Bernard, "The divine nature of Jesus is God the Father" [p]while His human nature is the flesh. [q]He states that Jesus is not another God or a part of God but the Father who puts on flesh as a man puts on coat to bridge the gap between man and God that man's sin created. [r]

In summary, the Holy Spirit first descend on Mary to set the platform for the successful fusion of God's Word with an egg in her womb, which lead to the formation of a living being, an ideal man who was supernaturally conceived and virgin born – Jesus of Nazareth, the Son of the living God.

THE WORD MADE FLESH

Just as God came from heaven to take the dust from the earth to make a body for the first Adam, the same process was applicable in the case of the last Adam because God revealed himself through his active power to take a seed from Mary. The seed is a type of the substance from the earth (the dust) he took in the beginning to prepare a body for Adam according to the Scripture that says our human body is made from the dust of the earth (Gen.3:19). Consequently, Jesus was fully God and man in essence because he had a complete human nature and a complete divine nature that perfectly fused and merged in him while on earth.

LESSONS

1. The Word of God truly became flesh and dwelt among us to save humankind from sin and death.

2. The key Scripture that helps to understand the mystery about his incarnation is Luke1:35.

3. The Holy Spirit had to first descend on Mary to set the platform for the successful fusion of God's Word with an egg in her womb.

4. The Word of God became human when he fused with an egg cell in Mary's womb.

5. The first Adam is a type of the last – Jesus of Nazareth, the Son of the living God.

6. God created a body for the first Adam because a spirit cannot live on earth without a body.

7. The body of the last Adam was prepared with the seed God took from Mary's womb on which resides humanity.

8. The principle established in the beginning demands that every living thing be born to gain legitimacy on earth.

9. God did not make his eternal Word jump out of eternity to time because he respects principles.

10. Mary played an important role in the process because: (a) she has an egg (ovum) that contains half of the genetic material known as DNA. (b) She has a womb where the fertilized ovum will be incubated for development and growth. (c) She is a descendant of Abraham. (d) She is a virgin. (e) She is a woman whose seed was going to bruise the head of the serpent.

11. Jesus was fully human and fully God while on earth because of his genetic makeup that was composed of both humanity and divinity. His cell contains copies of the gene in Mary's cell on which resides humanity and that of the eternal Word of God in which resides divinity.

12. His humanity is by incarnation while his deity is by virtue of his pre-existence as the Word of God.

13. Without incarnation, the legitimacy of his existence on earth as human will be questioned, thereby bringing him under a curse for breaking the rule of nature.

14. He is an ideal man that differs from other men because of his supernatural conception and virgin birth.

SIGNIFICANCE OF THE WORD BECOMING FLESH

1. The Word of God became flesh and dwelt among men to reconcile humankind to God through his sacrificial death on the cross of Calvary and his triumphant resurrection.

2. The humanity, sonship, lordship, kingship, priesthood of Christ and the divine sonship of a Christian are due to his incarnation (Hebrew2:9-10).

3. Through incarnation, God's Word met the lawful righteous requirements of the Father for the redemption and salvation of human race. He broke down the wall of hostility and tore the veil of limitation that existed between God and humankind.

4. By faith in his name, we humans can freely access the Godhead with confidence at any time and obtain things from him because of the work Christ accomplished in favor of humankind (Eph.2:18, 3:12).

5. The Word became flesh to bring humanity to oneness with the Father – the creator, sustainer and supreme governor of heaven and earth. He accomplished it by uniting himself to humans, and granting us eternal life being God's own life in order to make us one with the Father.

6. The Word became flesh that he may destroy the devil that holds the power of death and release those whose lives were in bondage through their fear of death (Heb.2:14-15).

7. The incarnation of God's Word was a positional change because he is by nature God, since he is one with the eternal Father in essence. He voluntarily stripped himself of all privileges, rights and dignity to become human and rescue humankind from the dominion of darkness.

8. The Father exalted Jesus above the heavens and earth because of what he did for humanity and gave him a name that is higher than every other name in heaven, on earth and beneath the earth. He also made him both Lord and Christ (Acts2:36, Phi.2:5-11).

9. While he was on earth, God commanded the angels to worship him; a privilege that is not given to any being other than God himself, who made it clear from the beginning that he will never share his glory, honor or worship with anyone (Ex.20:1-5,34:14).

10. The Godhead commanded angels to worship Jesus in his incarnate state because he was fully God, and man even though he took the nature of a servant (Heb.1:5-13).

DIFFERENCE
BETWEEN THE FIRST AND LAST ADAM

The first Adam is a created being because the Godhead made him in the beginning in his own image and likeness (Gen.1:26-28, 5:1-2), while the last Adam–Christ is a deity because he pre-exists in God in eternity past as part of his being. The name he is called from the beginning is the Word of God (Jn.1:1-4). He is one in essence with the Godhead.

The first Adam brought sin, condemnation, spiritual death, and destruction to humanity by transgressing the command of God in the beginning (Rom.5:12-21).The last Adam brought righteousness, justification, and immortality to humankind through his obedience to the will of God, and his atoning sacrifice by which he redeemed human souls from sin and death (Rom.5:15-21).

THE WORD MADE FLESH

The first Adam was made a living being according to the written word of God (1Co.15:45). The last Adam became a life-giving spirit, who brought life and immortality to light through his triumphant resurrection. He gives eternal life to human race in the light of the gospel message that is preached in his name (1Co.15:45-46).

The first Adam was of the dust of the earth (1Co.15:47). The last Adam is from heaven (1 Co.15:47).

The first Adam was merely a figure and pattern of what was to come (Rom.5:14). The last Adam – Christ is the real person, who was foreshadowed.

CHAPTER 4

JESUS OF NAZARETH

STUDY QUESTIONS

1. Who is Jesus?

2. What is the significant of his name?

3. How did he get the name Jesus of Nazareth, the Son of the living God?

4. How did he inaugurate a new era of God's kingdom on earth?

5. How was his divine sonship validated

6. How did he destroy the wall of hostility that stood between God and humanity?

7. How was the mortal component in his body transformed to immortality?

8. How will the mortal body of believers be clothed with immortality on the last day?

The name Jesus being the Greek equivalent of the Hebrew Joshua means, "The Lord saves or salvation is from Yahweh." It was the proper name given to the incarnate Word of God by the angel Gabriel even before Mary conceived him.

The ONENESS of GOD

The name reveals the nature of his person – a savior – and his mission on earth, which was to rescue and save lost humanity. The name also came because of the divine principle of naming things that God established in the beginning as means of identification that distinguished him from every other person.

But while he thought on these things, behold, the angel of the LORD appeared unto him in a dream, saying, Joseph, thou son of David, fear not to take unto thee Mary thy wife: for that which is conceived in her is of the Holy Ghost. And she shall bring forth a son and thou shalt call his name JESUS: for he shall save his people from their sins.
(Matt. 1:20-21 KJV)

You will be with child and give birth to a son, and you are to give him the name Jesus. He will be great and will be called the Son of the Most High. The Lord God will give him the throne of his father David, and he will reign over the house of Jacob forever; his kingdom will never end.
(Lk.1:31-33 NIV)

Matthew George Easton (author of *Easton's Bible Dictionary*) defines and describes the name as the Greek form of the Hebrew Joshua that was originally Hoshea but changed by Moses into Jehoshua or Joshua. He adds, "After the Exile, it assumed the form Jeshua, whence the Greek form Jesus. It was given to our Lord to denote the object of his mission, which was to save (Matt 1:21)." [a]

The name "Jesus" was, at the time of our Lord's earthly sojourn, among the most popular of names selected by parents of Hebrew boys. In the writings of the Jewish historian Josephus, the name identifies at least twenty different men, ten of whom were contemporaries of Jesus Christ.

JESUS OF NAZARETH

Its popularity was probably to a large extent due to its relationship with one of Israel's great leaders, Joshua, the son of Nun and successor to Moses. In the Egyptian papyri, the name occurs frequently right through the early part of the second century. Then abruptly, both Jews and Christians stopped using "Jesus" as a name for their boys. The Jews did so because it was so closely related to Christianity, which they rigorously opposed and hated. The Christians refused to use the name for opposite reasons. To them, the name was special and held in veneration. It was almost thought sacrilegious that anyone but Jesus should bear that name. [b]

About the name, Rev. Bernard writes, "The Old Testament promised   that there would come a time when Jehovah would have one name and that this one name would be made known (Zechariah14:9; Isaiah52:6). We know that the one name of Matthew28:19 is Jesus, for Jesus is the name of the Father (John5:43, Hebrew1:4), the Son (Matthew1:21), and the Holy Ghost (John14:26)." [c]

The name refers to the eternal Spirit of God (the Father) dwelling in the flesh. We can use the name Jesus to describe either one of His two natures or both. [d]

I must say here that Jesus is not God the Father neither is he the Holy Ghost but the Word of God that became flesh to rescue humanity from the power of darkness. He is a unique and an ideal man who differs from all other men because of his miraculous conception, virgin birth, and sinless nature.

The ONENESS of GOD

The Bible declares in 2Corintians 5:21 that God made him who had no sin to be sin on our behalf, so that we might become the righteousness of God in him. While 1Peter 2:22 says he committed no sin and no deceit was found in his mouth.

He was born by Mary, who was pledged to be married to Joseph in Bethlehem of Judea the city of king David as a descendant of his royal lineage because Joseph whom Mary was engaged to was from the house and lineage of king David (Lk.2:4-7). When he was born, his parents took him to their hometown Nazareth of Galilee, where he grew to adult. This is why he is called Jesus of Nazareth or Jesus the Nazarene.

And he went and lived in a city called Nazareth, that what was spoken by the prophets might be fulfilled: "He shall be called a Nazarene."
(Matt. 2:23 ESV)

In addition to his proper name, he was called the Son of God, a title that the angel Gabriel gave him before birth; hence the name "Jesus of Nazareth, the Son of the living God."

And behold, you will conceive in your womb and bring forth a Son, and shall call His name Jesus. He will be great, and will be called the Son of the Highest; and the Lord God will give Him the throne of His father David. And He will reign over the house of Jacob forever, and of His kingdom there will be no end.
(Lk. 1:31-33NKJV)

JESUS OF NAZARETH

When he was about thirty years old, he began his earthly ministry, which was preaching, and teaching about God and the kingdom of heaven with the intention of inaugurating a new era of God's kingdom on earth. He finally accomplished it through his sacrificial death on the cross of Calvary for the redemption of humankind. Through this, the human nature that constitutes part of his being, which he got from Mary, was transformed to supernatural by the power of the Holy Spirit. That is to say, the seed of death (mortal component) contained in his DNA changed to immortality when he rose triumphantly from death. As a result, he became a life-giving spirit because the mortality in his body was clothed with immortality.

There are also heavenly bodies and there are earthly bodies; but the splendor of the heavenly bodies is one kind, and the splendor of the earthly bodies is another. The sun has one kind of splendor, the moon another and the stars another; and star differs from star in splendor. So will it be with the resurrection of the dead. The body that is sown is perishable, it is raised imperishable; it is sown in dishonor, it is raised in glory; it is sown in weakness, it is raised in power; it is sown a natural body, it is raised a spiritual body. If there is a natural body, there is also a spiritual body. So it is written: "The first man Adam became a living being; the last Adam, a life-giving spirit."
(1Co.15:40-45 NIV)

It was necessary for the mortal component in his body to be clothed with immortality because flesh and blood cannot inherit the kingdom of God according to Scripture neither can the perishable inherited the imperishable, since he was to ascend bodily to heaven after resurrection.

The ONENESS of GOD

Brothers, I tell you this: flesh and blood cannot inherit the kingdom of God, and corruption cannot inherit in corruption. Listen! I am telling you a mystery: We will not all fall asleep, but we will all be changed, in a moment, in the twinkling of an eye, at the last trumpet. For the trumpet will sound, and the dead will be raised incorruptible, and we will be changed. Because this corruptible must be clothed with incorruptibility, and this mortal must be clothed with immortality. Now when this corruptible is clothed with incorruptibility, and this mortal is clothed with immortality, then the saying that is written will take place: Death has been swallowed up in victory.
(1Co.15:50-54HCSB)

The spiritual changes that occurred in his body set a precedent for what shall happen to the believers at his second coming when our mortal body shall be instantly clothed with immortality by the power of the Holy Spirit. This will happen at the sound of the trumpet call of God, with the voice of the archangel to meet the Lord in the cloud of glory.

For this we say to you by the word of the Lord, that we who are alive, and remain until the coming of the Lord, shall not precede those who have fallen asleep. For the Lord Himself will descend from heaven with a shout, with the voice of the archangel, and with the trumpet of God; and the dead in Christ shall rise first. Then we who are alive and remain shall be caught up together with them in the clouds to meet the Lord in the air, and thus we shall always be with the Lord.
(1Thes. 4:15-18 NASB)

ROMANS1:4

Paul, a servant of Christ Jesus, called to be an apostle and set apart for the gospel of God— the gospel he promised beforehand through his prophets in the Holy Scriptures regarding his Son, who as to his human nature was a descendant of David, and who through the Spirit of holiness was declared with power to be the Son of God by his resurrection from the dead: Jesus Christ our Lord. Through him and for his name's sake, we received grace and apostleship to call people from among all the Gentiles to the obedience that comes from faith. (Rom.1:1-6 NIV)

Scripture affirms in the above passage that Jesus was declared with power to be the Son of God by his resurrection from the dead. *The New Living Translation* says he was shown to be the Son of God when he was raised from the dead by the power of the Holy Spirit.

The Message puts it this way, "His unique identity as Son of God was shown by the Spirit when Jesus was raised from the dead, setting him apart as the Messiah, our Master." *The Amplified Bible* throws more light on it. It says, "And [as to His divine nature] according to the Spirit of holiness was openly designated the Son of God in power [in a striking, triumphant and miraculous manner] by His resurrection from the dead, even Jesus Christ our Lord (the Messiah, the Anointed One)."

This suggests that Jesus' divine sonship was revealed, proven and authenticated through resurrection, because it sets him apart as the Son of God (no human could have done what he did). He conquered death, and dominated the power of the grave.

He then ascended bodily to heaven, where the Father crowned him with glory and exalted him to the highest place of honor and dignity by given him a name that is above every other name. So that at the mention of his name – i.e. Jesus Christ, every knee should bow in heaven and on earth, and under the earth, and every tongue confesses that Jesus Christ is Lord to the glory of the Father (Acts 2:36).

Let this mind be in you which was also in Christ Jesus, who, being in the form of God, did not consider it robbery to be equal with God, but made Himself of no reputation, taking the form of a bondservant, and coming in the likeness of men. And being found in appearance as a man, He humbled Himself and became obedient to the point of death, even the death of the cross. Therefore God also has highly exalted Him and given Him the name which is above every name, that at the name of Jesus every knee should bow, of those in heaven, and of those on earth, and of those under the earth, and that every tongue should confess that Jesus Christ is Lord, to the glory of God the Father.
(Phil 2:5-11 NKJV)

Jesus did not become the Son of God because of his death and resurrection as many think and boldly affirm, since he exists as the Son of God from the moment he was born. To be precise, he became a Son through "incarnation" (Lk.1:31-33). However, his divine sonship was validated through the audible voice that came from the Father on the day he was Baptized (Matt.3:17), on the Mountain of Transfiguration (Matt.17:5), and through his resurrection, which is a proof of his deity (Rom.1:3-4).

Some do not agree with the above point of view, more especially the Oneness believers. To them, Jesus is the Son of God because the Spirit of God conceived him, making God his real father. Rev. Bernard puts it this way, "Jesus is the Son of God because God, and not a man, caused His conception. God was literally His Father." [e]

Finally, he ascended to heaven and sat at the right hand of the Majesty (Mk.16:19) in the courtroom of heaven as a mediator between the Godhead and humankind (1Tim.2:5). He gave eternal life to humanity, brought us to oneness with the Father, destroyed the existing dividing wall of hostility, and opened a new and living way for humanity through the veil into the most holy place by his eternal blood.

Therefore, brethren, since we have full freedom and confidence to enter into the [Holy of] Holies [by the power and virtue] in the blood of Jesus, By this fresh (new) and living way which He initiated and dedicated and opened for us through the separating curtain (veil of the Holy of Holies), that is, through His flesh, And since we have [such] a great and wonderful and noble Priest [Who rules] over the house of God (Heb.10:19-21 AMP)

LESSONS

1. Jesus is the Son of God and the Son of Man that gave himself up as sin offering for the salvation of human race.
2. His name reveals the nature of his person – a savior – and his mission on earth, which was to rescue and save lost humanity.

3. He pre-existed as the Word of God. He became both the Son of God and the Son of Man through incarnation and a life giving spirit by virtue of his resurrection.

4. He is neither God the Father nor the Holy Spirit but the Son of God and the Son of Man.

5. He was born by the Virgin Mary in Bethlehem as a descendant of King David royal lineage.

6. He grew from childhood to adult in a town called Nazareth of Galilee as a Nazarene – hence the name Jesus of Nazareth or Jesus the Nazarene.

7. He was also called the Son of God, a name or title that the angel Gabriel gave him before birth; hence the name Jesus of Nazareth, the Son of the living God.

8. He inaugurated a new era of God's kingdom on earth through his sacrificial death and triumphant resurrection.

9. The Father confirmed his divine sonship at Baptism, and Transfiguration. It was also validated through his resurrection, which was a proof of his deity.

10. When he rose from the dead, his mortal body was clothed with immortality and he became a life-giving spirit before ascending to heaven because flesh and blood cannot inherit the kingdom of God.

11. He ascended bodily to the right-hand throne of the Majesty in the courtroom of heaven to mediate for humankind.

CHAPTER 5

THRONE OF GRACE

STUDY QUESTIONS

1. What is the throne of grace all about?

2. Where is it located?

3. On what is it founded?

4. Who sits on it?

5. Why was it established by the Godhead?

6. What other names can this throne be called?

7. How important is the throne of grace in the heavenly courtroom to humankind?

8. What differentiate it from the other thrones in heaven?

9. Can a believer exercise dominion mandate on earth as Christ does in heaven?

10. If yes, in what measure or proportion will the person's spiritual authority be?

The ONENESS of GOD

Therefore, since we have a great high priest who has gone through the heavens, Jesus the Son of God, let us hold firmly to the faith we profess. For we do not have a high priest who is unable to sympathize with our weaknesses, but we have one who has been tempted in every way, just as we are—yet was without sin. Let us then approach the throne of grace with confidence, so that we may receive mercy and find grace to help us in our time of need.
(Heb.4:14-16 NIV)

Before the incarnation of God's Word, an everlasting promise was made to King David that one of his seeds would reign eternally sitting on his throne, and that the priest will never fail to have someone to continually offer burnt offerings and sacrifice to God. For this sure word of promise to be fulfilled, God planned to cause a Righteous Branch to spring up from the lineage of King David that will do what is just and right in the land. The name by which he will be called is, "The LORD Our Righteousness."

Behold, the days are coming,' says the LORD, 'that I will perform that good thing which I have promised to the house of Israel and to the house of Judah: ' In those days and at that time I will cause to grow up to David A Branch of righteousness; He shall execute judgment and righteousness in the earth. In those days Judah will be saved, And Jerusalem will dwell safely. And this is the name by which she will be called: THE LORD OUR RIGHTEOUSNESS.' "For thus says the LORD: 'David shall never lack a man to sit on the throne of the house of Israel; nor shall the priests, the Levites, lack a man to offer burnt offerings before Me, to kindle grain offerings, and to sacrifice continually."
(Jer. 33:14-18 NKJV)

THRONE OF GRACE

When the angel Gabriel brought the news about Jesus' birth to Mary in Luke1:31-33, he said she would give birth to a son who was to be named Jesus. He adds that the child will be great and called the Son of the Most High, for the Lord God will give him the throne of his ancestor David on which he will reign over the house of Jacob forever. This then means that the long awaited descendant of King David who was to reign on his throne continually according to the promise of God was Jesus of Nazareth, the Son of the living God. He is the incarnate Word of God, who became Lord and Christ because of his atoning sacrifice (Acts.2:36).

Having accomplished his redemptive work on earth, he sat as king and priest over the house of God (heaven), on the eternal throne promise to the seed of King David. This was done to fulfill the promise God made to the house of Israel by establishing one of their sons as eternal king and priest in his presence. The very throne on which Jesus Christ, who died and rose for the sins of the world, sits in the heavenly throne room is called the "Throne of Grace."

The throne of grace is therefore, the only platform in the heavenly courtroom that a living soul can step into by faith in Christ Jesus and obtain mercy from the Godhead because the one sitting on it is the man Jesus Christ, who went to represent humanity in the heavenly courtroom as a mediator between God and human race. The Bible declares in 1Timothy 2:5 that there is only one God, and only one mediator between God and humankind, the Man Christ Jesus. The apostle Paul also writes in Romans 8:34 that Christ is at the right hand of God interceding for us.

The ONENESS of GOD

The throne of grace is a seat of honor, glory, blessings, sovereign power, and authority established on "Grace and Truth." A living soul can boldly approach it by faith and prayer, and obtain one blessing after another in Christ. In addition, the mediation activity of Christ between the Godhead and humanity is put to effect on this very throne. The throne is next to the supreme authority in the heavenly throne room called the Mercy Seat, on which the Godhead sits as Father over all things (I'll expand on this as we proceed). That is to say, after the Godhead in the courtroom of heaven, the next person in hierarchy is Jesus of Nazareth, the Son of Man. The presence of this throne in the heavenly courtroom encourages the believers to enter with boldness and full assurance of faith in Christ Jesus. Because he opened for us a new and living way to the Father through the curtain, i.e., his body and he lives forever to intercede and save whoever comes to the Father through him.

But He, because He continues forever, has an unchangeable priesthood. Therefore He is also able to save to the uttermost those who come to God through Him, since He always lives to make intercession for them. For such a High Priest was fitting for us, who is holy, harmless, undefiled, separate from sinners, and has become higher than the heavens.
(Heb.7:24-26 NKJV)

The throne of grace is a throne that is located at the center of the heavenly courtroom, which is also the very place where the throne of the Godhead is situated.

THRONE OF GRACE

For the Lamb in the midst of the throne will be their shepherd, and he will guide them to springs of living water, and God will wipe away every tear from their eyes."
(Rev.7:17 ESV)

For this reason, it is refers to as the right-hand throne of the Majesty or the throne at the right hand side of the Godhead in the middle of the heavenly courtroom. The four living creatures and twenty-four elders surround both the throne of the Godhead and the throne of the lamb, which are the mercy seat and the throne of grace.

Then I saw a Lamb, looking as if it had been slain, <u>standing in the center of the throne,</u> encircled by the four living creatures and the elders. He had seven horns and seven eyes, which are the seven spirits of God sent out into all the earth. He came and took the scroll from <u>the right hand of him who sat on the throne.</u> And when he had taken it, the four living creatures and the twenty-four elders fell down before the Lamb. Each one had a harp and they were holding golden bowls full of incense, which are the prayers of the saints.
(Rev.5:6-8 NIV)

RIGHT HAND OF GOD

Adam Clarke explains, "The right hand was considered as the most noble, and the instrument of conveying the highest dignities, and thus it has ever been considered among all nations, though the reason of it is not particularly obvious. Even in the heavens the right hand of God is the place of the most exalted dignity." [a]

The ONENESS of GOD

From biblical point of view, the "right hand" speaks of power, strength, authority and prominence. A good example is a story in Genesis48:13-19, which talks about how Joseph brought his two sons Manasseh and Ephraim to his father Jacob so he may bless them. He positioned Ephraim, who was his younger son in his right hand and directed him toward his father's left hand, and he used his left hand to direct Manasseh (his firstborn) toward Jacob's right hand. When Jacob stretched out his right hand to bless them, he crossed his arm and put the right hand on the head of Ephraim, and his left hand on Manasseh's head, even though he was the firstborn.

When Joseph saw that his father Jacob laid his right hand on the head of Ephraim, he was displeased. So he lifted his father's hand to move it from Ephraim's head and place it on the head of Manasseh. Joseph said to him, "No, my father, this one is the firstborn; put your right hand on his head." But his father refused to remove his right hand from the head of Ephraim, and by the laying on of his right hand, he conferred on Ephraim, the rights, privileges, and dignity of the firstborn.

And Joseph took them both, Ephraim in his right hand toward Israel's left hand, and Manasseh in his left hand toward Israel's right hand, and brought them near him. And Israel stretched out his right hand and laid it on the head of Ephraim, who was the younger, and his left hand on the head of Manasseh, crossing his hands (for Manasseh was the firstborn). And he blessed Joseph and said, "The God before whom my fathers Abraham and Isaac walked, the God who has been my shepherd all my life long to this day, the angel who has redeemed me from all evil, bless the boys; and in them let my name be carried on,

and the name of my fathers Abraham and Isaac; and let them grow into a multitude in the midst of the earth." When Joseph saw that his father laid his right hand on the head of Ephraim, it displeased him, and he took his father's hand to move it from Ephraim's head to Manasseh's head. And Joseph said to his father, "Not this way, my father; since this one is the firstborn, put your right hand on his head." But his father refused and said, "I know, my son, I know. He also shall become a people, and he also shall be great. Nevertheless, his younger brother shall be greater than he, and his offspring shall become a multitude of nations."
(ESV)

The Bible declares in Exodus15:6 that the right hand of God is great in power and that his right hand shattered the enemies while Psalms118:15-16 says the right hand of God does mighty things.

Shouts of joy and victory resound in the tents of the righteous: "The Lord's right hand has done mighty things! The Lord's right hand is lifted high; the Lord's right hand has done mighty things!"
(Ps.118:15-16NIV)

From our previous note on the eternal power of God, we discover that it is synonymous with the right hand of God, which then means that God's right hand speaks of his power, might and authority. The right hand of God is a figurative expression that signifies God's sovereign power because he exercises his authority by his right hand. Psalms 21:8 says the Lord's right hand will find those who hate him.

To be at the right hand of God therefore means to be position or established by his sovereign power.

The ONENESS of GOD

1Peter 3:22 says Christ went to heaven and he is at the right hand of God; angels, authorities, and powers are made subject to him. This implies that where Christ sits in heaven is a place of dignity and sovereign power that the angels, authorities and powers submit to him.

Before Jesus ascended to heaven, he said in Matthew 28:18 that all power in heaven and on earth has been given to him. Acts 2:33 says God exalted him to his right hand, while Philipians 1:20 declares that God sat him at his right hand in the heavenly realms. The Godhead exalted Christ to the highest place of dignity and placed him above all rule and authority, power and dominion, titles and names. He puts all things under his authority and appointed him head in everything to the church.

When Christ left the Godhead as his Word to become flesh, he was a spirit being but when he ascended back to heaven, he went with a glorified human body to represent humankind in heaven. Hebrew 12:2, says because of the joy that was set before him, he endured the cross, despised the shame and sat down at the right hand of the throne of God. The Bible also declares in Matthew 25:31 that when he shall come in his glory, he will sit on his throne in heavenly glory (meaning he has a throne on which he sits in heaven).

The Godhead granted him this throne in the courtroom of heaven so he can mediate for humankind. This is why Daniel 7:13 says the Son of Man came with the clouds of heaven and approached the Ancient of Days.

Verse 14 adds that he was given authority, glory and sovereign power; all people worshipped him, while is dominion and kingdom is one that shall not end. Christ got the throne, glory, authority, sovereign power or dominion and kingdom from the Godhead when he ascended to heaven.

In my vision at night I looked, and there before me was one like a son of man, coming with the clouds of heaven. He approached the Ancient of Days and was led into his presence. He was given authority, glory and sovereign power; all peoples, nations and men of every language worshiped him. His dominion is an everlasting dominion that will not pass away, and his kingdom is one that will never be destroyed. (Dan 7:13-14NIV)

HOW MANY THRONES ARE THERE IN HEAVEN

In Revelation4:2-3, John saw a throne in heaven on which someone sat but he could not give a visual picture of the one sitting on it because Scripture tells us he lives in unapproachable light and that no one can see his face and live (1Tim.6:15-16, Ex.33:20, Jn.1:18, 1Jn.4:12). All John could do is to say someone sits on the throne instead of revealing the exact picture of the person. The Bible declares in Revelation 4:5 that from the throne come flashes of lightning, rumblings and pearls of thunder. Verse 8 reveals that the one sitting on the throne is the Lord God Almighty who was (speaks of the past), and who is (indicates the present), and who is to come (signifies the future)." If he is the past, present and future, it means he is eternal.

The ONENESS of GOD

Immediately I was in the Spirit, and there in heaven a throne was set. One was seated on the throne, and the One seated looked like jasper and carnelian stone. A rainbow that looked like an emerald surrounded the throne. Around that throne were 24 thrones, and on the thrones sat 24 elders dressed in white clothes, with gold crowns on their heads. From the throne came flashes of lightning, rumblings, and thunder. Burning before the throne were seven fiery torches, which are the seven spirits of God. Also before the throne was something like a sea of glass, similar to crystal. In the middle and around the throne were four living creatures covered with eyes in front and in back. The first living creature was like a lion; the second living creature was like a calf; the third living creature had a face like a man; and the fourth living creature was like a flying eagle. Each of the four living creatures had six wings; they were covered with eyes around and inside. Day and night they never stop, saying: Holy, holy, holy, Lord God, the Almighty, who was, who is, and who is coming. Whenever the living creatures give glory, honor, and thanks to the One seated on the throne, the One who lives forever and ever, the 24 elders fall down before the One seated on the throne, worship the One who lives forever and ever, cast their crowns before the throne, and say: Our Lord and God, You are worthy to receive glory and honor and power, because You have created all things, and because of Your will they exist and were created.
(Rev. 4:2-11HCSB)

Yet again, in chapter 5:1 and 7, John acknowledged the present of someone on the throne but he still could not figure out the exact image of the person. Verse 13 describes how every creature in heaven, on earth, in the sea and beneath sings to the one who sits on the throne and to the Lamb (sees also Rev.6:16, 7:10).

THRONE OF GRACE

The Scripture says the earth and sky flees from the presence of the one who sits on the great white throne (Rev.20:11). Whereas, the throne of the Lamb is the eternal throne promised to King David that Christ will sit on during his millennial reign (Rev.20:1-7). How then will Christ reign on earth for a thousand years if he is the one whose presence causes the earth and sky to flee? The answer is very simple because Scripture made it clear that Christ is not the Father. The one sitting on the throne whose image or face John could not depicts is the Godhead and he is the one whose presence causes the earth and sky to disappear. The throne on which he sits is called the great white throne or the mercy seat.

And I saw an angel coming down out of heaven, having the key to the Abyss and holding in his hand a great chain. He seized the dragon, that ancient serpent, who is the devil, or Satan, and bound him for a thousand years. He threw him into the Abyss, and locked and sealed it over him, to keep him from deceiving the nations anymore until the thousand years were ended. After that, he must be set free for a short time. I saw thrones on which were seated those who had been given authority to judge. And I saw the souls of those who had been beheaded because of their testimony for Jesus and because of the word of God. They had not worshiped the beast or his image and had not received his mark on their foreheads or their hands. They came to life and reigned with Christ a thousand years. (The rest of the dead did not come to life until the thousand years were ended.) This is the first resurrection. Blessed and holy are those who have part in the first resurrection. The second death has no power over them, but they will be priests of God and of Christ and will reign with him for a thousand years.

The ONENESS of GOD

And when the thousand years are ended, Satan will be loosed from his prison and will come out to deceive the nations which are at the four corners of the earth, that is, Gog and Magog, to gather them for battle; their number is like the sand of the sea. And they marched up over the broad earth and surrounded the camp of the saints and the beloved city; but fire came down from heaven and consumed them, and the devil who had deceived them was thrown into the lake of fire and sulphur where the beast and the false prophet were, and they will be tormented day and night for ever and ever. Then I saw a great white throne and him who sat upon it; from his presence earth and sky fled away, and no place was found for them. And I saw the dead, great and small, standing before the throne, and books were opened. Also another book was opened, which is the book of life. And the dead were judged by what was written in the books, by what they had done. And the sea gave up the dead in it, Death and Hades gave up the dead in them, and all were judged by what they had done. Then Death and Hades were thrown into the lake of fire. This is the second death, the lake of fire; and if any one's name was not found written in the book of life, he was thrown into the lake of fire.

(Rev. 20:1-12 RSV)

Acts 7:55-56 reveals how Stephen saw God's glory and Jesus standing at his right hand. Like John, he could not also give a visual picture of God when the heaven opened, instead he saw his splendor for no human could see God and live. That is why Christ is the exact representation of his being to humanity so that whoever sees Jesus sees the Father (Heb. 1:3, Jn. 14:9).

But he, full of the Holy Spirit, gazed into heaven and saw the glory of God, and Jesus standing at the right hand of God. And he said, "Behold, I see the heavens opened, and the Son of Man standing at the right hand of God."
(Acts 7:55-57ESV)

In conclusion, there are two thrones in the center of the heavenly courtroom. Twenty-four other thrones on which twenty-four elders dressed in white with crowns of gold on their heads sit surround the two thrones. The Godhead and Jesus Christ sit on them. That is why Bible passages like Revelation5:13, 6:16, 7:10, 21:22, 22:1 and 3 talk about God and the Lamb or rather the throne of God and the Lamb. However, these two thrones is considered as one because Christ is an extension of God's being and whatever he has, belong to the Father (Jn.15:16).

The Lord Jesus promised in Revelation3:21 to give whoever overcomes the right to sit with him on his throne just as he overcame and sat with his Father on his throne. That is to say, though there are two thrones namely: the throne of God on which the Godhead sits and the throne of the Lamb on which Christ sits, the two are one because God and Christ are one indivisible and inseparable being. Jesus said in John 10:30, "I and the Father are one." (See also Jn.17:11, 22)

OTHER NAMES
FOR THE THRONE OF GRACE

1 - Throne of the Son of God: the Son of the living God — Jesus Christ of Nazareth, sits on this throne in the heavenly courtroom as priest and king over the house of his Father.

The ONENESS of GOD

The Bible declares in Hebrew 1:8 that about the Son he says, "Your throne, O God, will last forever and ever, and righteousness will be the scepter of your kingdom. Chapter 5:5 says Christ did not take it upon himself to become High Priest but he was chosen by God who said to him, "You are my son. Today I have become your father."

2 - Throne of the Son of Man: after his death and resurrection, the Lord Jesus ascended bodily to heaven as the Son of Man and sat on it to mediate between the Godhead and humanity. The Prophet Daniel says in chapter 7:13-14 that as he was watching in the night visions, he saw someone like a son of man coming with the clouds of heaven and he approached the Ancient of Days. He adds that the person was escorted into the presence of the Godhead where he received glory, a kingdom and the authority to rule, so that people from every nation and language should serve him. His dominion is an endless one that will not pass away, while his kingdom is the type that will not be destroyed.

3 - Throne of the Lamb: the lamb is the figurative name given to the incarnate Word of God because of his sacrificial work on the cross. He got the throne from the Father because of the redemptive work he accomplished in favor of the human race (Rev. 22:1 and 3).

4 - Judgment Seat of Christ: on the last day, the believers in Christ shall present themselves before it and be rewarded according to the work they did while on earth, which the Bible declares in Revelation14:13 will follow them. This means that Christians will not face the great white throne judgment that will be administered to those whose names are not written in the Lamb's book of life.

THRONE OF GRACE

In Paul's second letter to the believers in Corinth, he said in chapter 5:10 that we must all appear before the judgment seat of Christ that each one may receive what is due them for the things done on earth, whether good or bad.

5 - Right-hand Throne of the Majesty: this glorious throne that is located at the right hand of the Godhead in the middle of the heavenly throne room is the highest place of power and authority in the courtroom of heaven after the Mercy Seat, on which the eternal Father sits (Lk.22:69, Mk.14:62, Heb.1:3).

6 - Eternal Throne Promised to the Seed of David: Jesus Christ got this eternal throne promised by the Godhead to his ancestor, King David because he is the Righteous Branch that sprang from his lineage to rule over his house forever. Luke confirms this in chapter1:32-33 when he says the Lord God will give Jesus the throne of his father David, and that he will reign over the house of Jacob forever.

In summary, the throne of grace is the second highest place of honor, dignity, glory, power, and authority in the heavenly courtroom. It is next to the Mercy Seat which is the throne of the Godhead—the supreme authority. God's dominion was entrusted to Jesus who sits on it when he inherited all things from the Father. So that all may honor the Son just as they honor the Father and whoever does not honor the Son, does not honor the Father that sent him.

The Father judges no one, but has given all judgment to the Son, that all may honor the Son, just as they honor the Father. Whoever does not honor the Son does not honor the Father who sent him.
(Jn.5:22-23 ESV)

The ONENESS of GOD

He commanded us to preach to the people and to testify that he is the one whom God appointed as judge of the living and the dead. All the prophets testify about him that everyone who believes in him receives forgiveness of sins through his name.

(Acts 10:42-43NIV)

In these last days, he has spoken to us by [His] Son, whom he has appointed heir of all things and through whom he made the universe. He is the radiance of His glory, the exact expression of His nature, and He sustains all things by His powerful word. After making purification for sins, He sat down at the right hand of the Majesty on high.

(Heb.1:2-3 HCSB)

This throne is the only platform in the heavenly courtroom that a living soul can approach by faith in Christ Jesus, and pray to obtain things from the Father in times of need because the one sitting on it tore the veil of hindrance and opened a living way for humankind to the Father. He also established believers as co-heir with himself of all things including the throne of grace – a spiritual platform that is higher than all rules, powers, authorities and dominion in heaven, on earth and beneath the earth.

Praise be to the God and Father of our Lord Jesus Christ, who has blessed us in the heavenly realms with every spiritual blessing in Christ. For he chose us in him before the creation of the world to be holy and blameless in his sight in love.

(Eph.1:3, 4 NIV)

THRONE OF GRACE

Even when we were dead in trespasses, made us alive together with Christ (by grace you have been saved), and raised us up together, and made us sit together in the heavenly places in Christ Jesus, that in the ages to come He might show the exceeding riches of His grace in His kindness toward us in Christ Jesus.
(Eph.2:4-7 NKJV)

With true knowledge and understanding of Scripture, a Christian can exercise the same authority and dominion by faith and prayer as Christ does in heaven. This would be in the measure or proportion of revelation knowledge of the written word of God that the individual has about Jesus Christ, because the Father gives us everything that pertains to life and godliness to enjoy, through the knowledge we have about him and his Son Jesus Christ (2Pet.1:2-3).

It was on this throne that Christ received the promised Holy Spirit and poured him out on the sons of men for spiritual regeneration.

God has raised this Jesus to life and we are all witnesses of the fact. Exalted to the right hand of God, he has received from the Father the promised Holy Spirit and has poured out what you now see and hear.
(Acts.2:32-33 NIV)

This then means that God's unmerited gifts, blessings and favor are given to the sons of men in Christ from this throne. The absence of this throne in the courtroom of heaven would mean spiritual death and destruction for humankind, because our divine sonship and heirship is due to the presence of Christ and the throne of grace in the heavenly courtroom.

With these in mind, we cannot help saying "thank you" to God and Father of our lord and savior Jesus Christ, for the throne of grace in the heavenly courtroom and the Lamb who sits on it to mediate for humankind.

LESSONS

1. The throne of grace is a seat of honor, glory, blessings, sovereign power, and authority established on grace and truth.

2. The throne is the only platform in the courtroom of heaven that a living soul can approach by faith in Christ Jesus, and pray to obtain things from the Father in times of need.

3. The throne is next to the supreme authority in the heavenly throne room called the mercy seat, on which the Godhead sits as Father over all things.

4. The presence of this throne in the heavenly courtroom encourages the believers to enter with boldness and full assurance of faith in Christ Jesus.

5. The mediation activity of Christ for humanity is put to effect on this very throne.

6. The throne is located at the center of the heavenly courtroom, which is also the very place where the throne of the Godhead is situated.

7. The four living creatures and twenty-four elders surround both this throne and that of the Godhead.

THRONE OF GRACE

8. It was on this throne that Christ received the promised Holy Spirit and poured him out on humanity for spiritual birth.

9. The throne can also be refers to as the throne of the Son of God, the throne of the Son of Man, the throne of the Lamb, the right-hand throne of the Majesty, the eternal throne promised to the seed of David and the judgment seat of Christ.

10. God's unmerited gifts, blessings and favor are given to humans in Christ from this throne.

11. The divine sonship and heirship of a Christian is due to the presence of Christ and this throne in the heavenly courtroom.

CHAPTER 6

FATHER'S REWARD

STUDY QUESTIONS

1. What did the Father give to Jesus for the great work he accomplished for humanity?

2. What are the constituents of this reward?

3. Why was it given to Jesus of Nazareth?

4. Does God reward every good work we do?

The Father's reward consists of the immense treasure that Jesus of Nazareth, the Son of God received after he ascended bodily to the courtroom of heaven, because of his atoning sacrifice by which he redeemed people from every tribe and made them priests and kings to serve his father. He was officially attributed "power, riches, wisdom, strength, honor, glory, and blessing" by the Father who appointed him head in all things for the church (Eph. 1:21-23).

And they sang a new song, saying, Thou art worthy to take the book, and to open the seals thereof:

for thou wast slain, and hast redeemed us to God by thy blood out of every kindred, and tongue, and people, and nation; And hast made us unto our God kings and priests: and we shall reign on the earth. And I beheld, and I heard the voice of many angels round about the throne and the beasts and the elders: and the number of them was ten thousand times ten thousand, and thousands of thousands; Saying with a loud voice, Worthy is the Lamb that was slain to receive power, and riches, and wisdom, and strength, and honour, and glory, and blessing. And every creature which is in heaven, and on the earth, and under the earth, and such as are in the sea, and all that are in them, heard I saying, Blessing, and honour, and glory, and power, be unto him that sitteth upon the throne, and unto the Lamb forever and ever.
(Rev.5:9-13 KJV)

What we do see is Jesus, who was given a position "a little lower than the angels"; and because he suffered death for us, he is now "crowned with glory and honor." Yes, by God's grace, Jesus tasted death for everyone."
(Heb.2:9-NLT)

Jesus of Nazareth was highly honored by the Father in the heavenly throne room with these seven attributes that constitute what I call "The Father's Reward" and it consists of the following:

Glory – the throne of grace or the throne of the Son of God – (Heb.1: 8, 1Pet.3:22), as earlier mentioned could also be referred to as the right hand throne of the Majesty. It is the highest place of authority, power and dignity in the heavenly courtroom, subsequent to the mercy seat (the throne of the Majesty) because it ranks second. Jesus of Nazareth got it by right when he ascended to heaven.

FATHER'S REWARD

Riches – heir of all things – (Heb.1:2), having accomplished all things for humanity on earth through his redemptive work, the Godhead appointed him heir of all things whether visible or invisible.

Wisdom – manifold wisdom – (Col.2:2-3), the Bible declares that in Christ Jesus are hidden all the treasures of wisdom and knowledge, and that the manifold wisdom of God is unveiled to the rulers and authorities in the heavenly realms through the church – his body.

Power – lordship – (Acts2:36), because of his death and triumphant resurrection for the justification and redemption of humankind, the Godhead made him lord – that is to say, he puts all things under his authority and appoints him head in everything for the church (Eph.1:22). The apostle Paul writes in Romans 14:9 that the reason Christ died and returned to life is so that he might be the Lord of both the dead and the living. Jesus said in Matthew 28:18 that all authority in heaven and on earth has been given to him.

Honor – names and titles – (Acts2:36), because of his redemptive work, the incarnate Word of God was honored and crowned by the Father who gave him a glorious name (Jesus), made him Christ, and declared him his Son – Jesus Christ, the Son of the living God (Phi.2:9-11, Heb.1:4-6).

Strength – Holy Spirit – the psalmist says the hand of God Almighty (which speaks of his power) would rest on the man at his right hand whom he raised up for himself. "Let your hand rest on the man at your right hand, the son of man you have raised up for yourself." (Ps.80:17 NIV) Jesus Christ of Nazareth, the incarnate Word of God, is the man at the right hand side of the Father according to Scripture.

The ONENESS of GOD

He obtained the promised Holy Spirit (God's eternal active power) from the Father, and poured him out on the sons of men (Acts2:33). This is why the Bible sometimes refers to Jesus as the possessor of the sevenfold spirit of God (Rev.3:1, 5:6). While the Holy Spirit is sometimes called the Spirit of Christ or the Spirit of the Son of God (Phi.1:19, Rom.8:9, Gal.4:6), because the Father caused him – i.e. the Holy Spirit to dwell in the person of Jesus Christ his Son.

Blessing – the Book of life – (Rev.13:8), is also referred to as the Lamb's Book of Life, and is the only book in heaven on which the names of the redeemed are written. The only person authorized to inscribe the names of people on this book is the Lamb of God, who is Jesus Christ, the author and finisher of our faith (Rev.21:27).

LESSONS

1. The father's reward has to do with the great treasure that Jesus of Nazareth received from the Father when he ascended to heaven.

2. He got it because of his atoning sacrifice for human salvation.

3. God rewarded Christ because he did a good work for humanity.

4. The fact he was rewarded is an indication that God rewards every good work.

5. Galatians 6:9 says we should not become weary in doing good for at the proper time, we will reap a harvest if we do not give up.

6. The reward consists of the following: glory (the throne of grace), riches (heirs of all things), wisdom (manifold wisdom), power (lordship), honor (names and titles), strength (Holy Spirit) and blessing (the book of life).

CHAPTER 7

THE HOLY SPIRIT

STUDY QUESTIONS

1. Who is the Holy Spirit?

2. Where does he live?

3. Why did Christ pour him out on humans?

4. Did God prepare a special body for him to dwell in when he came out from him?

5. Why is he called the Spirit of Christ or the Spirit of the Son of God?

6. Why does the Scripture declare that in Christ dwells the fullness of the Deity?

7. Why is the throne of grace the habitation of God's living power?

8. How did God's Word and Spirit came together to form a single divine person?

Much has already been said about the Holy Spirit being God's eternal active power that enables him to do things. When we say the "Spirit of the Lord or Holy Ghost," it is another way of saying the "Holy Spirit."

The ONENESS of GOD

He subsisted in the Godhead in the beginning as a distinct being until the ascension of Jesus of Nazareth to the right hand throne of the Majesty where he (Jesus) received him (Holy Spirit) from the Father and poured him out on the sons of men (Acts.2:33) for spiritual regeneration and to execute God's agenda for humanity. From that moment, the Holy Spirit moved from the Godhead and resided in the person of Jesus Christ.

Without the Holy Spirit, God's divine agenda for humankind cannot be accomplished on earth. Likewise, without the human body, the Holy Spirit cannot work legally in this world, because the earth is not meant for spirit beings but humans. In as much as humans need God to do certain things on earth, God needs us to achieve his plans in the earth. The reason for this is that God gave the earth to humans, made it their domain, and excluded himself in the management and governance of earthly affairs (Gen.1:26 and Ps.115:16).

I believe one of the reasons the Lord said in Joel2:28 that he would pour out his Spirit on all flesh (people), and make our sons and daughters prophecy, while our old men will dream dreams, and our young men see visions, is that the human body keeps the Holy Spirit legal on earth to achieve God's agenda. Otherwise, God would only make him hover over the face of the earth as he did in Genesis1:2 rather than making him dwell in it. The Holy Spirit could not dwell on earth because there was no human vessel (body) to live in at the time, since human was not yet created.

THE HOLY SPIRIT

For him (Holy Spirit) to live on earth, he needs human body to resides in and work through, reason why Christ poured him out on humans to regenerate our spirit from spiritual death that came on humankind in the beginning through the sins of Adam. Second, that he may transform us into Christ perfect image in words and deeds, though faith and revelation knowledge of God's word.

Speaking about the Holy Spirit in John 14:17, the Lord Jesus said the world couldn't accept him because it neither sees him nor knows him. Nevertheless, the disciples knew him because he lived with them, and he would be in them. 1 Corinthians 3:16 says we are God's temple and that God's Spirit dwells in us. Chapter 6:18 warns us to avoid sexual sin because it defiles our body, and makes it inappropriate for the Holy Spirit to live in. Verses 19 and 20 inform us that our body is the temple of the Holy Spirit, who lives in us, and that we do not own ourselves for we were bought with a price. We have to honor God with our bodies by living a life of holiness so his Spirit can dwell in us.

Flee from sexual immorality. All other sins a man commits are outside his body, but he who sins sexually sins against his own body. Do you not know that your body is a temple of the Holy Spirit, who is in you, whom you have received from God? You are not your own; you were bought at a price. Therefore honor God with your body.
(1 Co. 6:18-20NIV)

Oneness believers see the Holy Spirit as another term for the one God. Rev. Bernard explains in his book that the term emphasizes a particular aspect of God.

The ONENESS of GOD

In addition, he writes, "When we speak of the Holy Spirit, we are reminding ourselves of God's invisible work among men and of His ability to anoint, baptize, fill and indwell human lives." To conclude, he said the term speaks of God in activity. [a]

Oneness theology maintains that the Holy Spirit is none other than God the Father. Rev. Bernard puts it this way, "The Holy Spirit is none other than Jehovah God and none other than the Father." [b]To him, the phrase "Spirit of the Lord" merely emphasizes that the Lord God is indeed a Spirit rather than a distinction of persons in the Godhead. He argues, "It does not suggest a plurality of persons any more than when we speak of a man's spirit." [c]

The Spirit of the Lord is not a separate entity or deity but a part of God's being that he granted the right to subsist as individual being, though with one essence because of his eternal plan that he programmed before the world began. The plurality of persons in the Godhead is not to be taken for separate deities uniting under the umbrella of Godhead for that would imply polytheism (the worship or belief in many gods or divinities). Instead, it reveals the fact that though God is indivisibly one, he granted his eternal power the right to subsist as individual being in him, and it subsisted as his Word and Spirit.

Unlike God's Word, for whom a body was supernaturally prepared when he left the Godhead to live among men, the Holy Spirit was not given a special body. Instead, he resides in the person of Jesus Christ. This is why Scripture refers to him as the Spirit of Christ or the Spirit of the Son of God.

WORD AND SPIRIT OF GOD

The Word of God and the Spirit of God are the two components of God's living power coming together in the person of Jesus Christ to form a divine being. Jesus in who resides the person of the Holy Spirit is the embodiment of God's eternal power, which is the first constituents of God. For this reason, Scripture declares that the fullness of the Deity dwells in the person of Christ because the sum of all that make up the Godhead are his eternal power, and divine nature that now resides in Christ Jesus.

As you therefore have received Christ Jesus the Lord, so walk in Him, rooted and built up in Him and established in the faith, as you have been taught, abounding in it with thanksgiving. Beware lest anyone cheat you through philosophy and empty deceit, according to the tradition of men, according to the basic principles of the world, and not according to Christ. For in Him dwells all the fullness of the Godhead bodily; and you are complete in Him, who is the head of all principality and power.
(Col 2:6-10 NKJV)

Oneness believers interpret this passage of the Bible differently. To them, it means the Father, Son, Holy Ghost, Jehovah, Word and so on, are all in Jesus. [d] I would like to point out that God is a spirit with individuality, intellect, emotion, will, and personality. His eternal power and divine essence constitute the fullness of his being in eternity past (Rom.1:20). The beginning commenced when he granted his eternal power the right to exist as individual being, and it subsisted in him as his Word and Spirit (Jn.1:1).

The ONENESS of GOD

At the fullness of time (Gal.4:4), his Word became flesh (Jn.1:14), died (Acts2:23), rose (Acts2:24), ascended bodily to heaven (Mk.16:19), obtained the Holy Spirit (Acts2:33) and sat at his right hand (Eph.1:20) to mediate for humankind (1Tim2:5).

The incarnation of God's Word is an extension of his being in human form. That is why God and his Word remain indivisible and inseparable from each other. Hebrew 1:3 says Jesus is the exact representation of God's image because everything that makes up the Godhead namely: his Word, Spirit and essence are all embodied in him so that whoever sees him sees the Father that sent him, for he is no different from the Father (Jn.14:8-11). We must understand also that no human can see the Godhead and live according to Scripture (1Tim.6:15-16, Ex.33:20), because the earth and sky flee from his presence but Jesus Christ shall come to reign on earth for a thousand years (Rev.20:1-7). That is to say, Jesus is not the Father even though the fullness of the Godhead is embodied in him.

Before the incarnation of God's Word – Jesus of Nazareth, the Holy Spirit descended to put God's plan and counsel to effect in the life of Mary, which eventually led to his miraculous conception. During Jesus earthly ministry, he also descended on him according to Scripture to help him accomplish the mission he received from the Father (Lk.1:31-35, 4:18-19, Matt.12:28).

The person (being) of the Holy Spirit is made up of his divine nature (essence) and power, which are revealed to humans in presence and power. However, before a person can have a tangible experience of this power and presence of the Holy Spirit, he or she must believe in Jesus Christ, the Son of God.

THE HOLY SPIRIT

Oneness teaching asserts that the Holy Spirit is merely the title of God in action rather than a divine being. They affirm that the Father, Son and Spirit are three distinct ways through which the one God successively manifests himself to save human race. That is to say, the Father is both the Son and the Holy Spirit and that the three do not simultaneously coexist. They dispute and reject the concept of individuality and subsistence as regards to the Holy Spirit holding that God is indivisibly one and that he manifest in whatever way he pleases, and that the Holy Spirit is nothing more or less than one of the ways he chooses to reveal himself to humankind.

While commenting on a phrase in Isaiah48:16 that says, "...the Lord God, and his Spirit hath sent me," Rev. Bernard mentions, "Lord God" means the sum total of God in all His glory and transcendence, while "his Spirit" refers to that aspect of Him with which the prophet has come into contact and which has moved upon the prophet." Furthermore, he quoted Isaiah63:7-11 and 14 to prove his stand against distinction of persons between God and His Spirit adding that the Lord is a Spirit and the Spirit of the Lord is simply God in action. [e]

Today, the Holy Spirit resides and subsists in the person of Christ to bring about the fullness of God's eternal power, which is the very first between the two fundamental constituent attributes of God. The throne of grace been the highest place of honor and dignity in the heavenly throne room subsequent to the mercy seat, becomes the habitation of the fullness of God's eternal power in the embodiment of Christ.

The ONENESS of GOD

For this reason, Scripture declares in Colossians 1:19 that it pleases the Father so well to have all his fullness (namely his Word, Spirit, and Essence) dwells in Christ, so that in all things, he may have preeminence.

> Which He brought about in Christ, when He raised Him from the dead and seated Him at His right hand in the heavenly places, far above all rule and authority and power and dominion, and every name that is named, not only in this age but also in the one to come. And He put all things in subjection under His feet, and gave Him as head over all things to the church, which is His body, the fullness of Him who fills all in all. (Eph.1:20-23 NASB)

Although God's Word and Spirit have both manifested respectively at different times in history and in divers ways, they now reside in the person of Jesus Christ.

LESSONS

1. The Holy Spirit is God's eternal active power that enables him to do things.

2. He subsisted in the Godhead as a distinct being until the ascension of Jesus to the right hand throne of the Majesty.

3. He now resides and subsists in the person of Jesus to bring about the fullness of God's eternal power in the embodiment of Christ.

4. The Lord Jesus poured him out on humans for spiritual regeneration and transformation.

5. A special body was not prepared for him when he emanated from the Godhead to reside in the person of Christ.

THE HOLY SPIRIT

6. The Holy Spirit is called the Spirit of Christ because Jesus got him from the Godhead as a result of his redemptive work for humanity.

7. The fullness of the Deity dwells in the person of Christ because the totality of the Godhead, which is composed of his eternal power and divine nature, resides in him.

8. The throne of grace is the habitation of God's eternal power since the Word and Spirit of God that make up his eternal power are embodied in Christ who sits on it.

9. God's Word and Spirit came together in the person of Christ to form a divine being.

CHAPTER 8

GREAT WHITE THRONE

STUDY QUESTIONS

1. What is the great white throne all about?

2. On what is it founded?

3. Where is it located?

4. Who sits on it?

5. Why is it reserved for the last and final judgment?

6. Why is it greater than the throne of grace?

7. Why is the throne called the mercy seat?

8. How did the Godhead inhabits the throne in the beginning?

9. Why will this throne and the throne of grace be the supreme authority in the New Jerusalem?

Then I saw a great white throne and him who was seated on it. Earth and sky fled from his presence, and there was no place for them. (Rev.20:11NIV)

As explained in chapter 6, the great white throne is the supreme authority and the highest place of honor, dignity, glory, and power in the heavenly throne room. Psalms 89:14 says righteousness and justice are the foundation of this throne, while mercy resides on it.

The ONENESS of GOD

From the throne comes flashes of lightening, rumblings and peals of thunder (Rev.4:5). The eternal self-existent, self-sufficient, all-powerful transcendent God from whom all things derived existence sits on it, while twenty-four other thrones on which twenty-four elders dressed in white with crowns of gold on their heads sit surround this throne (Rev.4:2-4).

The throne can also be called the mercy seat, which was the gold-cover of the Ark of the Covenant that contained the stone tablet of the covenant, the gold jar of manna and Aaron's staff that budded. Above it were the cherubim of glory that overshadowed it.

... the ark of the covenant overlaid round about with gold, wherein was the golden pot that had manna, and Aaron's rod that budded, and the tables of the covenant. And over it the cherubim of glory shadowing the mercy seat; of which we cannot now speak particularly.
(Heb.9:4-5 KJV)

The stone tablets of the covenant present in the ark highlights the sovereignty and supremacy of the Godhead, while the gold jar of manna points to the Word of God that became flesh — Jesus of Nazareth. He died for the sin of humanity and rose triumphantly for our justification, after which he ascended back to heaven and sat on the throne of grace. Aaron's staff that budded speaks of God's active power that also emanated from him to live in the person of Jesus Christ, on the throne of grace.

If these three items namely:

1. The stone tablets of the testimony, which speaks of the sovereignty of God

GREAT WHITE THRONE

2. The gold jar of manna that points to the Word of God

3. Aaron's staff that budded, which symbolizes the active power of God also known as the Holy Spirit

Were all in the ark of covenant that was covered by the mercy seat in the most holy place, it stands to reason that God, his Word, and Spirit inhabit this throne in the beginning as a single unit or divine being. This was before his Word, and Spirit came out of him to exist as distinct divine beings in Christ.

The Godhead who sits on the great white throne, placed all things under the feet (authority) of Jesus Christ, and appointed him head in all things for the church (Eph.1:20-22). For this reason, we are encouraged in the Scripture to come to the throne of grace with confidence, by faith in Christ Jesus to obtain mercy and find grace to help in times of need (Heb.4:15-16).

The great white throne is also called the throne of the ancient of days that flames with fire. A fiery stream goes forth from before it. Thousands upon thousands of people attend him, while ten thousand times ten thousand stand before him. The Prophet Daniel writes in chapter 7:9-10 of his book that as he looked in a night vision, thrones were set in place, and the Ancient of Days took his seat. His clothing was as white as snow and the hair of his head white like wool. His throne flames and its wheels were all ablaze. A river of fire flows out from before him. Thousands upon thousands attended him and ten thousand times ten thousand stood before him. The court sat and the books were opened.

He adds in verses 26 and 27 that the power of the beast will be taken away from him and destroyed while, the whole kingdom under heaven will be handed over to the people of the Most High, so that everyone may worship and obey the Ancient of Days whose kingdom is everlasting.

LAST AND FINAL JUDGMENT

This throne is reserved for the last and final judgment that shall be administered to the dead on the last day. It is called the "Great White Throne Judgment." This shall happen when the dead, great and small whose names are not written in the Book of Life of the Lamb will be judged according to what they have done, as it is recorded in the books. The sea would give up the dead in it, death and Hades would give up the dead that are in them so that all may appear before this throne. Death and Hades will be thrown into the lakes of fire been the second death, and any one whose name is not written in the book of life would be thrown into the lake of fire too.

The earth and sky flee from the presence of this throne and the one who sits on it, whose face or image no human can depicts since none can see him and live. Only on the last day when flesh would have given way for the spirit will this throne appear to judge the dead according to their deeds while alive as recorded in the books.

Then I saw a great white throne and Him who sat on it, from whose face the earth and the heaven fled away. And there was found no place for them. And I saw the dead, small and great, standing before God, and books were opened.

GREAT WHITE THRONE

And another book was opened, which is the Book of Life. And the dead were judged according to their works, by the things which were written in the books. The sea gave up the dead who were in it, and Death and Hades delivered up the dead who were in them. And they were judged, each one according to his works. Then Death and Hades were cast into the lake of fire. This is the second death. And anyone not found written in the Book of Life was cast into the lake of fire.
(Rev.20:11-15 NKJV)

This whole thing will take place when Christ hands over the kingdom to God the Father after destroying all dominion, authorities and power according to Scripture. His reign will continue until he puts all his enemies under his feet and the very last enemy to be destroyed is death. After that, the Son would become subject to him who puts all things under his feet, so that God may be overall. When Scripture says that all things are put under Christ, it is evident that it does not include the Father who put all things under his authority because the Father is greater than the Son is.

You heard me say, 'I am going away and I am coming back to you.' If you loved me, you would be glad that I am going to the Father, for the Father is greater than I.
(Jn.14:28 NIV)

Therefore, a time is coming when Christ would hand all things over to the Father. Then whoever, whether male or female whose name is not written in the Book of Life of the Lamb would appear before the Father on the great white throne to be judged according to their works as it is written in the books of record.

The ONENESS of GOD

Meanwhile, those whose names are written in the Book of Life would enter the New Jerusalem – the City of God (Rev.21:22-27), and be rewarded by Christ who sits on the throne of grace, for the work they accomplished on earth in his name. Just as the Father is greater than the Son is, so is the great white throne greater than the throne of grace.

Then comes the end, when He hands over the kingdom to God the Father, when He abolishes all rule and all authority and power. . For He must reign until He puts all His enemies under His feet. The last enemy to be abolished is death. For He has put everything under His feet. But when it says "everything" is put under Him, it is obvious that He who puts everything under Him is the exception. And when everything is subject to Him, then the Son Himself will also be subject to Him who subjected everything to Him, so that God may be all in all.
(1Co.15:24-28 HCSB)

All we shall have in the end is the throne of God, on which the eternal Lord and creator of heaven and earth sits, and the throne of the Lamb on which the Lord Jesus Christ, the Son of the living God sits as king, priest and lord. The person of the Holy Spirit resides in Christ according to the eternal plan and will of the Father. Thus, the "mercy seat" and the "throne of grace" on which God and his Son Jesus sit shall be the supreme authority for eternity in the new heaven and earth.

The Lord Jesus said in John 8:17-18 that according to the Law, the testimony of two men is valid. He is one who testifies for himself and his other witness is the Father that sent him.

GREAT WHITE THRONE

This means that Jesus is not the Father, and the Father is not Jesus. The Bible affirms in 2Corinthians 1:3 and 11:31 that the Godhead is the God and Father of Jesus Christ, while Jesus is his Son (Jn.3:16). The throne of grace is not the throne of the Ancient of Days or the mercy seat, just as Jesus Christ is not the Godhead. Although, the two thrones are one just as God and Christ is indivisibly one in essence. For that reason, you see the Bible use the singular "throne" rather than the plural "thrones" as in the Scriptures below.

> Then the angel showed me the river of the water of life, as clear as crystal, flowing from the throne of God and of the Lamb. (Rev.22:1NIV)

> I saw no temple in the city, for the Lord God Almighty and the Lamb are its temple. And the city has no need of sun or moon, for the glory of God illuminates the city, and the Lamb is its light. (Rev.21:22-23 NLT)

LESSONS

1. The great white throne is the supreme authority in the courtroom of heaven.

2. Righteousness and justice are its foundation, while mercy resides on it.

3. It is located at the middle of the heavenly courtroom while twenty-four other thrones on which twenty-four elders dressed in white, with crowns of gold on their heads sit surround it.

4. The throne is the seat of the all-sufficient and self-existent God whose reign and dominion is from eternity to eternity.

5. The throne is also called the mercy seat and the throne of the Ancient of days that flames with fire, while a fiery stream goes out from before it.

6. The throne is greater than the throne of grace because the one sitting on it is the God and Father of Jesus Christ who sits on the throne of grace.

7. The Godhead inhabits this throne in the beginning as God, his Word, and Spirit before sending his Word to die for human sins.

8. It is reserved for the final judgment that shall be administered to the dead on the last day.

9. This throne and the throne of grace shall be the supreme authority in the New Jerusalem because they are the seats of the Godhead, and Jesus Christ his Son.

10. Any man or woman whose name is not written in the Book of Life of the Lamb shall appear before this throne on the last day to be judge according to their deeds as recorded in the books.

CHAPTER 9

FATHERHOOD OF GOD

STUDY QUESTIONS

1. What does it mean to say that God is a father?

2. Why does Scripture refer to him as the Father of Christ?

3. Why is he the Father of all existing things?

4. How significant is the fatherhood of God over Christ?

5. What do the fatherhood of God and the sonship of Christ imply?

To speak of God as a father in general terms has to do with his sovereignty, supremacy and headship over all things because nothing exists outside him. All things begin and end in him. For this reason, Scripture refers to him as the Alpha and Omega, the Beginning and End, the First and the Last (Is.44:6, Rev.21:6).

According to the *Dictionary of Bible Themes*, the fatherhood of God "primarily signifies his paternal relationship to Jesus Christ. The term also refers to God's fatherly relationship to his creation, especially to believers as the 'children of God." [a]

The ONENESS of GOD

2Corinthians1:3 refers to him as the God and Father of our lord Jesus Christ; the Father of mercy and God of all comfort, while Hebrew2:10 tells us that all things exist through him and for him, thereby making him the source of whatever exists.

The same dictionary refers to him as, "the creator and redeemer of the world, who reveals himself in Scripture, in Jesus Christ, and who is loved, worshipped, and adored by believers. He is the Father of Jesus Christ and of all believers." [b] The apostle Paul puts it this way; there is one God and Father of all, who is over all and through all, and in all (Eph.4:6).

Oneness believers use the word "Father" in relation to God to emphasize his role as creator, Father of spirits, Father of the born-again believers and the Father of the humanity of Jesus Christ. [c] According to them, there is only one Father and Jesus is the one Father. [d]

The Bible declares in 1Corinthians8:6 that there is only one God, the Father who created everything, and we live for him; there is only one lord Jesus Christ, through whom God made everything and through whom we have been given life. From this Scripture, we understand that all things derive existence from God because he created them for his own glory, which then made him the source of whatever exists. Revelation4:11 declares, "You are worthy, our Lord and God, to receive glory and honor and power, for you created all things, and by your will they were created and have their being." (NIV)

GOD AND FATHER OF JESUS CHRIST

Apart from the fact God is the Father of all things, the Bible repeatedly affirms that he is the God and Father of our lord Jesus Christ (Rom.15:6, 2Co.11:31), while Jesus is declared the Son of God (Gal.4:4, Heb.1:5, 1Jn.2:22-25). The fatherhood of God and the sonship of Christ reveal the father and son relationship in the Godhead.

The fatherhood of God over Christ and the divine sonship of Jesus is a very important subject to the body of Christ. However, many in the Christendom hold different opinions, as not all have reached a consensus on the true meaning and significant of the subject since the beginning of church history. Some argue that Christ was eternally begotten, holding that the conception and virgin birth did not make him the Son of God. To them, there was never a time when he was not the Son of God. He was, is and will forever remain the Son of God. Others hold one of the following views:

1. He became the Son of God through incarnation.

2. He was declared the Son of God through resurrection.

3. He became God's Son at baptism.

4. He became God's Son when he ascended to heaven.

5. He became God's son after God created him.

Hebrew 1:5 says, "For to which of the angels did God ever say, "You are my Son; today I have become your Father or again, "I will be his Father, and he will be my Son." (NIV) Chapter 5:5 also declares, "… he was chosen by God, who said to him, "You are my Son. Today I have become your Father." (NLT) We discover from these two passages that before the incarnation of God's Word, the principle of divine sonship was in place.

However, it was not put to effect in connection with the Godhead. For God to say concerning his Son "you are my son; <u>today</u> I have become your father" or again, "<u>I will</u> be his father and <u>he will be</u> my son," means that he had it as a plan from the beginning; but waited until the fullness of time for his Word to be incarnated (Gal.4:4). The word <u>today</u> in the passage implies a specific day or time, contrary to the popular notion of divine sonship called "eternal generation" as it relates to the Son of God. The reason for this is that sonship implies a father, which highlights the idea of generation (a stage in the lineage of a family history when it all starts). The plan God had from the beginning as regard to sonship became a reality when he finally caused his Word to become flesh at a specific point in time and lived among humans.

When the angel Gabriel brought the news about the incarnation of God's Word to Mary, he said, "he shall be called the son of the Most High," meaning before then, he exists only as the Word of God rather than a Son. Through incarnation, the Word of God stripped himself of all divine privileges, rights and dignity to become the Son of God, while God himself became a father to the incarnate Word (Lk.1:31-32, Jn1:14). This means that the Word of God was not eternally begotten as God's Son. He got the rights of Son in relation to God and Man through incarnation.

According to Finis Dake, Bible passages like Ps.2:7, 12, Matt.1:18-25, Lk.1:35, Heb.1:5-6 etc. reveal that God was to have a Son and the Son a Father on a certain day in the future from the time the Prophets spoke.

FATHERHOOD OF GOD

He adds, "If sonship refers to deity, then this deity had a beginning on a certain day and He was not eternal. But if it refers to humanity, then all Scripture are clear and we have no man-made mystery of the so-called eternal sonship of Jesus Christ. If it refers to both deity and humanity, then when did He become God, when was He begotten, how could He have been eternal?" [e]

Multiplied problems increase and become unanswerable with Scripture if we hold to the theory of eternal sonship, but all questions are clear when we accept the plain statements of Scripture that sonship refers to humanity and not to deity. [f]

The doctrine of <u>eternal sonship</u> of Jesus Christ is irreconcilable to reason, is unscriptural, and is contradictory to itself. Eternity has no beginning, so if He has been God from eternity, then He could not have a beginning as God. Eternity has no reference to <u>time,</u> so if He was begotten "THIS DAY," then it was done in time and not in eternity. [g]

Adam Clarke writes, "...the doctrine of the eternal Sonship of Christ is, in my opinion, anti-scriptural, and highly dangerous. This doctrine I reject for the following reasons:

1. I have not been able to find any express declaration in the Scriptures concerning it.

2. If Christ be the Son of God as to his divine nature, then he cannot be eternal; for son implies a father; and father implies, in reference to son, precedency in time, if not in nature too. Father and son imply the idea of generation; and generation implies a time in which it was effected, and time also antecedent to such generation.

3. If Christ be the Son of God, as to his divine nature, then the Father is of necessity prior, consequently superior to him.

4. Again, if this divine nature were begotten of the Father, then it must be in time; i.e. there was a period in which it did not exist, and a period when it began to exist. This destroys the eternity of our blessed Lord, and robs him at once of his Godhead.

5. To say that he was begotten from all eternity, is, in my opinion absurd; and the phrase eternal Son is a positive self-contradiction. Eternity is that which has had no beginning, nor stands in any reference to time. Son supposes time, generation, and father; and time also antecedent to such generation. Therefore the conjunction of these two terms, Son and eternity is absolutely impossible, as they imply essentially different and opposite ideas." [h]

Oneness theology also rejects the doctrine of eternal sonship stating that the Son is not eternally begotten, but that he came into actual or substantial existence at the incarnation when the Spirit of God conceived him. [i] According to them, the Father is not the Son, but the deity in the Son is the Father. "Since Jesus is the name of the Son of God, both as to His deity as Father and as to His humanity as Son, it is the name of both the Father and the Son." [j]

In contrast to Oneness doctrine that claims Jesus is both the Father and the Son, the Bible clearly highlights distinction of persons between the two, even though they are one in essence. The fatherhood of God over Jesus Christ reveals his sovereignty, supremacy and headship as the source from which Christ emanated because he subsisted in him – i.e. the Godhead in the beginning as his Word.

FATHERHOOD OF GOD

As I explained before, the word "father" implies source, and to call the Godhead the Father of our Lord Jesus means he is the source where Christ came from. Jesus Christ, the incarnate Word of God came out of God's eternal power in eternity, and subsisted in the Godhead as distinct being, which made the Godhead to give him the name "Word of God" in keeping with his divine principle of naming things as a way of differentiating him from other beings that later came into existence.

The Godhead begot him in eternity past as his "Word" not a "Son," and planned to make him a Son one day according to Hebrew1:5 and 5:5, where he said, "you are my son; today I have become your father" or again, "I will be his father and he will be my son." This means that Christ has a source since he originated from the Godhead, first as his Word in eternity, and then as a Son in time.

In his first epistle to the Corinthians, chapter 11:3, the apostle Paul writes, "But there is one thing I want you to know: The head of every man is Christ, the head of woman is man, and the head of Christ is God." (NLT) He also refers to the Godhead as the God and Father of Jesus Christ (2Co.11:31).

The Godhead is God and Father to Jesus Christ because Christ is an extension of his being. The Father is his source. He was begotten in eternity past from God's eternal power as the "Word of God," which marked the beginning of God's works (the act of transitioning from simply being an aspect of God's eternal power to exist independently as God's Word commenced the beginning of God's works in eternity past).

The ONENESS of GOD

The reason John1:1 says in the beginning was the Word, the Word was with God, and the word was God, is that he began the beginning. Verse 2 adds, "He was with God in the beginning." (For more information on this, please go to chapter 2).

He became a Son through incarnation at a specific time in history. He was born by Mary in Bethlehem of Judea the city of King David as a descendant of his royal lineage, and he grew up in a town name Nazareth in Galilee, Israel. He was one of the composition elements of God's eternal power in eternity past; he became the "Word of God" in the beginning (still in eternity since God's activities began in eternity and continuous forever), and then the Son of God on a particular day in time through incarnation. Without the Godhead, there is no Christ, and without Christ, the Godhead is not complete, since Christ is part of his being.

Grace, mercy, and peace will be with you from God the Father and from the Lord Jesus Christ, the Son of the Father, in truth and love. (2Jn.1:3 NKJV)

The Father and Son relationship between the creator of heaven and earth, and Jesus of Nazareth is due to the oneness that exists between them both from the beginning and the eternal plan of the Godhead that was accomplished in Christ. This means that though he made himself nothing by taking on the very nature of a servant to redeem humankind, he is one with the Godhead in essence based on his pre-existence.

In conclusion, the fatherhood of God and the sonship of Christ is an expression of God's love and divine purpose, which he accomplished in Jesus Christ – the incarnate Word.

FATHERHOOD OF GOD

The Bible declares in John 3:16 that God so loved the world he gave his one and only Son to die for the sins of humanity, so that whoever believes in him will not perish but have eternal life. Ephesians1:3-4 says, "Blessed be the God and Father of our Lord Jesus Christ, who hath blessed us with all spiritual blessings in heavenly places in Christ: According as he hath chosen us in him before the foundation of the world, that we should be holy and without blame before him in love." (KJV)

LESSONS

1. The fatherhood of God in general has to do with his headship over all things because nothing exists outside him whether visible or invisible. He is our source.

2. The fatherhood of God over Christ highlights his sovereignty and headship as the source from which Christ derived existence because he is part of God, and he subsisted in him (Godhead) as his Word in the beginning.

3. The fatherhood of God and the sonship of Christ reveal the father and son relationship in the Godhead.

4. The fatherhood of God and the sonship of Christ is an expression of God's love and divine purpose for humanity.

5. The Father and Son relationship between the creator of heaven and earth, and Jesus of Nazareth is due to the oneness that exists between them both from the beginning and the eternal plan of the Godhead for humankind, which he accomplished through Jesus Christ.

6. The Word of God was not eternally begotten as God's Son. He got the rights of Son in relation to God and Man through incarnation.

7. He was one of the composition elements of God's eternal power in eternity past; he became the "Word of God" in the beginning, and then the Son of God on a particular day in time through incarnation.

8. Without the Godhead, there is no Christ, and without Christ, the Godhead is not complete, because Christ is part of his being.

CHAPTER 10

DIVINE SONSHIP

STUDY QUESTIONS

1. What is divine sonship?

2. Why is Christ called a Son?

3. What is the nature of his sonship?

4. What is the basis for his sonship?

5. On what ground is a person declared son of God?

6. How important is this subject to the body of Christ?

The sonship of Christ, nature of his sonship, the basis for his sonship and the sonship of a Christian in connection with the Godhead is one of the major questions people ask in the Christendom. Although, much work has been done on the subject in some denominations, a lot remain undone because of the wide spread confusion among believers about it. I believe the church has come to a time when in-depth revelation knowledge of God's word on this subject is required to clear the ground of confusion, which the wicked have used to manipulate the lives and destinies of many Christians.

The ONENESS of GOD

But when the completion of the time came, God sent His Son, born of a woman, born under the law, to redeem those under the law, so that we might receive adoption as sons.
(Gal.4:4-5 HCSB)

Therefore come out from them and be separate, says the Lord. Touch no unclean thing, and I will receive you. I will be a Father to you, and you will be my sons and daughters, says the Lord Almighty.
(2Co. 6:17-18 NIV)

The Bible describes in Acts 8:26-40 how Philip was instructed by an angel of the Lord to go south down the desert road that runs from Jerusalem to Gaza where he met the official in charge of all the treasury of the queen of the Ethiopians. The Ethiopian eunuch, who went to Jerusalem to worship, was returning home sitting in his chariot as he reads aloud from the book of the Prophet Isaiah. Then the Holy Spirit asked Philip to go where the chariot was and stay near it. He ran over to where the man was and heard him reading from the book of Isaiah the prophet. Philip asked him whether he understood what he was reading. In response, the man said he could not unless someone explains it to him. Therefore, he asked Philip to come up into the chariot and sit with him so he could explain whom the prophet spoke about in the passage.

Now an angel of the Lord said to Philip, "Go south to the road — the desert road — that goes down from Jerusalem to Gaza." So he started out, and on his way he met an Ethiopian eunuch, an important official in charge of all the treasury of Candace, queen of the Ethiopians. This man had gone to Jerusalem to worship, and on his way home was sitting in his chariot reading the book of Isaiah the prophet.

DIVINE SONSHIP

The Spirit told Philip, "Go to that chariot and stay near it." Then Philip ran up to the chariot and heard the man reading Isaiah the prophet. "Do you understand what you are reading?" Philip asked. "How can I," he said, "unless someone explains it to me?" So he invited Philip to come up and sit with him. The eunuch was reading this passage of Scripture: "He was led like a sheep to the slaughter, and as a lamb before the shearer is silent, so he did not open his mouth. In his humiliation he was deprived of justice. Who can speak of his descendants? For his life was taken from the earth." The eunuch asked Philip, "Tell me, please, who is the prophet talking about, himself or someone else?" Then Philip began with that very passage of Scripture and told him the good news about Jesus. As they traveled along the road, they came to some water and the eunuch said, "Look, here is water. Why shouldn't I be baptized?" And he gave orders to stop the chariot. Then both Philip and the eunuch went down into the water and Philip baptized him. When they came up out of the water, the Spirit of the Lord suddenly took Philip away, and the eunuch did not see him again, but went on his way rejoicing. Philip, however, appeared at Azotus and traveled about, preaching the gospel in all the towns until he reached Caesarea. (NIV)

We discover in the above passage that though the man read about Christ, he could not understand until Philip explained the mystery to him. The apostle Paul writes in 1 Corinthians 2:6-8 that we speak God's wisdom in a mystery among those who are mature, a wisdom that the rulers of this age cannot understand. It takes revelation knowledge of God's word to unfold the mystery of the kingdom of heaven for a carnal mind cannot understand spiritual things.

The ONENESS of GOD

In verse 14, he adds that a person who is not spiritual cannot accept the things that come from the Spirit of God; for they are foolishness to him neither can he understand them because they are spiritually discerned. Without revelation knowledge of God's word, we cannot understand the things that relate to God and the kingdom of heaven.

Having read the works of others and heard many speak on the subject of divine sonship from different angle; it appears there is nothing more to add to what has been done. However, I pray that the Holy Spirit use this book and that of other people who are doing tremendous work on the subject in some denominations to enlighten the church and expand the boundary of understanding on the mystery of Christ and the church.

To start with, I would like to ask some questions that may possibly pave way for better understanding of the subject of divine sonship, its spiritual significance, and implication in relation to the Godhead.

1. Did Christ exist from eternity as the Son of God?

2. If yes, why would the angel Gabriel say to Mary that her child would be called "Son of God?"

3. Do you not think the angel should have rather said, "The Son of God" you are about to bring forth shall be called…?

4. Why is the incarnate Word of God called the "Son of God" and not something else?

5. The angel could have called him the friend of God, servant of God, lover of God and so on.

6. Why did angel Gabriel specify the word "Son" as relating to the incarnate Word?

DIVINE SONSHIP

7. What message was God passing across to humans by calling his incarnate Word, "A Son"?

8. What is the spiritual significance and implication of divine sonship?

9. How did Jesus of Nazareth become the Son of God?

10. Why is he called both the Son of God and the Son of Man?

From biblical point of view, divine sonship denotes legitimacy, oneness, and union with the Godhead. John5:17-18 reveals how the Jews tried to kill Jesus for calling God his own father. To them, Jesus statement implied equality with God. That is to say, for Jesus to call God his father literally means equality or oneness with him. For this, they got offended because they could not figure out the basis for the equality between Jesus of Nazareth and the Almighty God.

From biblical point of view, divine sonship denotes legitimacy, oneness, and union with the Godhead. John5:17-18 reveals how the Jews tried to kill Jesus for calling God his own father. To them, Jesus statement implied equality with God. That is to say, for Jesus to call God his father literally means equality or oneness with him. For this, they got offended because they could not figure out the basis for the equality between Jesus of Nazareth and the Almighty God.

Jesus said to them, "My Father is always at his work to this very day, and I, too, am working." For this reason the Jews tried all the harder to kill him; not only was he breaking the Sabbath, but he was even calling God his own Father, making himself equal with God. (Jn. 5:17-18NIV)

The ONENESS of GOD

Today, Christians come into oneness with God based on eternal life that is given to us for spiritual regeneration in Christ. This is done in the light of the gospel message been the word of truth that is preached in the name of Jesus, which produces faith for spiritual birth. Romans 10:17 says faith comes from hearing the good news about Christ. Once a living soul is born-again, the individual comes into union and oneness with the Godhead in Christ Jesus because of eternal life.

But what does it say? "The word is near you, in your mouth and in your heart" (that is, the word of faith that we proclaim); because, if you confess with your mouth that Jesus is Lord and believe in your heart that God raised him from the dead, you will be saved. For with the heart one believes and is justified, and with the mouth one confesses and is saved. For the Scripture says, "Everyone who believes in him will not be put to shame." For there is no distinction between Jew and Greek; the same Lord is Lord of all, bestowing his riches on all who call on him. For "everyone who calls on the name of the Lord will be saved." But how are they to call on him in whom they have not believed? And how are they to believe in him of whom they have never heard? And how are they to hear without someone preaching? And how are they to preach unless they are sent? As it is written, "How beautiful are the feet of those who preach the good news!" But they have not all obeyed the gospel. For Isaiah says, "Lord, who has believed what he has heard from us?" So faith comes from hearing, and hearing through the word of Christ. (Rom 10:8-17ESV)

DIVINE SONSHIP

Dake explains that sonship in connection with God had to refer to humanity and not to deity. He adds, "The word Son supposes time, generation, father, mother, beginning, and conception – unless one is a son by creation, as Adam (Lk.3:38), and angels (Job1:6; 2:1; Gen.6:1-4)." [a]

The writer of Hebrew highlights the peculiarity about the nature of the Son of God as follow, "..., like the Son of God he remains a priest forever." (Heb.7:3) From this passage, we understand that the Son of God posses' eternal life that makes him to live forever. When this life is given to a person in Christ Jesus by grace through faith, it brings the individual into union with the Godhead. That is why Ephesians 2:8 declares that we are saved by grace through faith.

But God, who is rich in mercy, out of the great love with which he loved us, even when we were dead through our trespasses, made us alive together with Christ (by grace you have been saved), and raised us up with him, and made us sit with him in the heavenly places in Christ Jesus, that in the coming ages he might show the immeasurable riches of his grace in kindness toward us in Christ Jesus. For by grace you have been saved through faith; and this is not your own doing, it is the gift of God - not because of works, lest any man should boast. For we are his workmanship, created in Christ Jesus for good works, which God prepared beforehand, that we should walk in them.
(Eph.2:4-10RSV)

John 1:12 says as many that received him and believed in his name, to them he gave the right to become the children of God. Verse 13 adds that they are children not born of flesh and blood but of God.

The free Online Dictionary defines sonship as "the state of being a son, or of bearing the relation of a son; filiation." [b] Romans10:9 declares that we shall be saved if we confess Jesus is Lord and believe that God raised him from the dead. Verse 10 says we believe with the heart to be justified, while we confess with the mouth to be saved.

He came to His own, and His own did not receive Him. But as many as received Him, to them He gave the right to become children of God, to those who believe in His name: who were born, not of blood, nor of the will of the flesh, nor of the will of man, but of God.
(John 1:11-13NKJV)

NATURE OF THE SONSHIP OF JESUS

STUDY QUESTIONS

1. Why does the Bible present Christ as the Son of God and the Son of Man?

2. How does the first differ from the latter?

3. What is the significant of Jesus divine and human sonship?

4. What is the basis for his human and divine sonship?

5. Why was it necessary for him to become both the Son of God and the Son of Man?

6. Could he have accomplished his mission without been both?

The sonship of Christ comes in two phases because Scripture presents him as the Son of God and the Son of Man. It therefore implies that he is both.

DIVINE SONSHIP

The former refers to his divine Sonship, while the latter refers to his human Sonship. Luke22:69-70 says, "But from now on, <u>the Son of Man</u> will be seated at the right hand of the mighty God." They all asked, "Are you then <u>the Son of God</u>?" He replied, "You are right in saying I am." (NIV)

But Jesus kept silent. And the high priest answered and said to Him, "I put You under oath by the living God: Tell us if You are the Christ, the Son of God!" Jesus said to him, "It is as you said. Nevertheless, I say to you, hereafter you will see the Son of Man sitting at the right hand of the Power, and coming on the clouds of heaven.
(Matt.26:63-64 NKJV)

To Rev. Bernard, the doctrine of the Son "teaches that God the Father so loved the world that He robed Himself in flesh and gave of Himself as the Son of God to reconcile the world to Himself (11Corinthians5:19). The one Jehovah God of the Old Testament, the great Creator of the universe, humbled Himself in the form of man so that man could see Him, understand Him, and communicate with Him. He made a body for Himself, called the Son of God." [c]

The Bible never said God the Father so love the world that he robed himself in flesh and gave himself off as the Son of God to reconcile the world to himself. Instead, it teaches that God so love the world that he gave his only begotten Son to save it. The Son of God is the incarnate Word (Jn.1:14), who gave himself off on the cross to reconcile the world to God the Father (2Co.5:18, Rom.8:3). Jesus is the incarnate Word of God. He pre-existed as the Word of God in the beginning. But when the fullness of time, which God appointed from the beginning came, he was made flesh through incarnation, and he became the Son of God to save humankind from sin (Matt.1:21).

DIVINE SONSHIP OF JESUS

(Jesus the Son of the living God)

STUDY QUESTIONS

1. How was Jesus divine sonship validated?

2. Why were the Jews offended at his claim to be the Son of God?

3. What does the concept of divine sonship mean to the Jews in Jesus time?

4. Why could they not accept him for whom he claimed to be?

5. Apart from the Godhead, did any other thing bear witness to Jesus' divine sonship?

6. Why do people still have the same problem that the Jews had with the divine sonship of Jesus?

This is how God showed his love among us: He sent his one and only Son into the world that we might live through him. This is love: not that we loved God, but that he loved us and sent his Son as an atoning sacrifice for our sins. And we have seen and testify that the Father has sent his Son to be the Savior of the world. If anyone acknowledges that Jesus is the Son of God, God lives in him and he in God.
(1Jn.4:9, 10, 14, 15 NIV)

The sonship of Jesus Christ in connection with the Godhead has to do with the equality and union that exist between both of them from the beginning because of Jesus pre-existence as God's Word, which constitutes the basis for his deity.

DIVINE SONSHIP

He is the firstborn of God according to Scripture, because the act of him transitioning from being one of the constituents of God's eternal power to individual subsistence in the Godhead marked the commencement of God's works, which in turns placed him above all things. This therefore made him head and first in the order of God's activities in eternity past. He was the first to obtain the right to exist as a distinct being in the Godhead, though with one essence, before any other thing came to existence (Col.1:15, Heb.1:6). The Bible refers to him as the one with God in the beginning or the one at the Father's side that revealed him to humans (Jn.1:1, 18). For more information on this, please go to chapter 2 and 3.

The pre-existence of Jesus of Nazareth as the Word of God is the basis for his equality with the Father, while his incarnation sets the platform for his divine sonship. It reveals the fact that though he became human, he remains one with the Godhead in essence.

According to Oneness theology, the term "Son of God" cannot be use apart from the humanity of Christ, for the word always refers to the flesh or the Spirit of God in flesh. (2) Son is always used with reference to time, for the Sonship had a beginning and will have an ending. (3) As God, Jesus had all power but as the Son He was limited in power." [d]

It is true that Jesus the incarnate Word became the Son of God through incarnation, but to say that his sonship will have an end is completely erroneous. The Bible teaches that Jesus remains both the Son of God and the Son of Man forever (it is indisputable).

The ONENESS of GOD

The angel does not give the appellation of Son of God to the divine nature of Christ; but to that holy person or thing, to hagion, which was to be born of the virgin, by the energy of the Holy Spirit. The divine nature could not be born of the virgin; the human nature was born of her. The divine nature had no beginning; it was God manifested in the flesh, 1 Tim 3:16; it was that Word which being in the beginning (from eternity) with God, John 1:2, was afterward made flesh (became manifest in human nature), and tabernacled among us, John 1:14. Of this divine nature the angel does not particularly speak here, but of the tabernacle or shrine which God was now preparing for it, namely the holy thing that was to be born of the virgin. Two natures must ever be distinguished in Christ: the human nature, in reference to which he is the Son of God and inferior to him, Mark 13:32; John 5:19; 14:28, and the divine nature which was from eternity, and equal to God, John 1:1; 10:30; Rom 9:5; Col 1:16-18. [ᵉ]

John10:24-39 recounts how the Jews gathered around Jesus and asked him, "How long will you keep us in suspense? If you are the Christ, tell us plainly." In response to their demand, Jesus said in verse 30, "I and the Father are one." At this, the Jews picked up stones to stone him, but he said to them in verse 32, "I have shown you many great miracles from the Father. For which of these do you stone me?" In response to his words, the Jews said in verse 33, "We are not stoning you for any of these, but for blasphemy, because you, a mere man, claim to be God." The Jews said all these because they could only see him from the human point of view as the son of a carpenter, having no knowledge of his pre-existence. For Jesus to confirm his claim and declaration as the Son of God, he refers them to the book of the law in the following verses of the Bible.

DIVINE SONSHIP

Jesus answered them, "Is it not written in your Law, 'I have said you are gods? If he called them 'gods,' to whom the word of God came—and the Scripture cannot be broken— what about the one whom the Father set apart as his very own and sent into the world? Why then do you accuse me of blasphemy because I said, 'I am God's Son'? Do not believe me unless I do what my Father does. But if I do it, even though you do not believe me, believe the miracles that you may know and understand that the Father is in me, and I in the Father." Again they tried to seize him, but he escaped their grasp.
(Jn.10:34-39 NIV)

From the above passage, we see how the Jews got upset at Jesus words and accuse him of blasphemy for claiming to be the Son of God. To them, the concept of divine sonship denotes equality with the Most High. However, at that time they could not figure out the possibility of Jesus been equal to him (Godhead), since they were ignorant of his pre-existence, which is the basis for Jesus' divine sonship and equality with the Father. Jesus did not refute or disapprove their accusation of him claiming equality with the Godhead by calling himself his Son. On the contrary, he drew their attention to the evidence that confirms his declaration in verse 36, where he refers to himself as the one whom the Father set apart as his very own, and sent into the world – a mystery that transcends their comprehension.

To further emphasis the significance and implication of his divine sonship, he said, "The Father is in me and I am in him." At this time, the Jews were mad at him and even attempted to kill him because they could not understand how the Godhead could be in Jesus the son of a carpenter, neither could they grasp how Jesus can be equal to the creator and lord of heaven and earth.

The ONENESS of GOD

Therefore, the Jews began persecuting Jesus because He was doing these things on the Sabbath. But Jesus responded to them, "My Father is still working, and I am working also." This is why the Jews began trying all the more to kill Him: not only was He breaking the Sabbath, but He was even calling God His own Father, making Himself equal with God.
(Jn.5:16-18 HCSB)

The same problem that the Jews had about the divine sonship of Jesus that hindered them from accepting him as the Son of God still exists because many have not come to the understanding of why he is equal to the eternal God. Until this is resolved through revelation knowledge of the word of God, the same problem will keep reoccurring and stopping people from accepting the truth about the person of Jesus Christ, as presented in the Bible for the salvation of human souls.

The Bible declares that God gave a divine order and commanded the heavenly host to worship him – a privilege that has never been given to anyone (Heb.1:5-6). Here, we see it given to Jesus of Nazareth because he is an extension of God. In addition, the sum of the constituent eternal qualities of God was embodied in him, which then made him a deity even while on earth.

Furthermore, the prophet Micah revealed the basis for his divine sonship many years before his birth in Bethlehem Judea as the ruler (shepherd) over the house Israel. According to him, his origin is from of old or ancient time–that is to say, eternity (Micah5:2).

DIVINE SONSHIP

For those who say Jesus divine sonship is due to his resurrection because of Romans1:4, which says he was declared with power to be the Son of God by his resurrection. I will start by saying that his resurrection played an important role in validating or confirming his divine sonship because his existence, which transcends time and mortality, was openly displayed through it. Only a deity could have done what he did, for he subdued and dominated death. Thus, the sonship of Jesus of Nazareth in regards to the Godhead is due to his pre-existence as the living Word of God that became flesh (go to chapter 3 for more information).

To Oneness believers, "Jesus is the Son of God because God, and not a man, caused His conception. God was literally His Father." [f]

Before his incarnation, he existed in eternity as the firstborn of God also known as the "Word of God" who became flesh (Heb.1:5-6, Jn.1:14). Through incarnation, he became the Son of God, and having been on earth for about thirty years, the Father spoke with a loud voice from heaven and confirmed his divine sonship on the day he was baptized (Lk.3:22). As he was about to end his earthly ministry, the Father again said in Matthew 17:5, "This is my son who I love, with him I am well pleased. Listen to him!" (NIV) This happened while he was on the mountain of transfiguration with his disciples.

Finally, Satan and unclean spirits bear witness to the divine sonship of Jesus several times in the Scripture (Mk.3:11-12, Matt.8:29, Lk.4:41).

In conclusion, the sonship of Jesus of Nazareth in relation to the Almighty God highlights the fact that though he made himself nothing by becoming flesh for the salvation of human souls, he holds equality with the Godhead in essence because he constitutes part of his being that pre-existed as his Word in the beginning.

HUMAN SONSHIP OF JESUS
(Jesus the Son of Man)

STUDY QUESTIONS

1. Why did Christ become the Son of Man?

2. How did his human sonship pave way for the divine sonship of Christians?

3. How did he destroy the wall of separation that stood between God and humankind?

4. How did he destroy the devil that holds the power of death and free those whose lives were in captivity for fear of death?

As it has been said earlier, the human sonship of the lord Jesus denotes equality and union with humankind. He pre-existed as the Word of God until the fixed time that the Godhead appointed for him to become one with humanity through incarnation. The reason for this is that the seeds of Abraham whom God made the promise to have flesh and blood, so the Word of God had to share in their human nature. He did so by becoming human like them, so that through death and resurrection, he might destroy the devil that holds the power of death and free those whose lives were in captivity for fear of death.

DIVINE SONSHIP

Since the children have flesh and blood, he too shared in their humanity so that by his death he might destroy him who holds the power of death—that is, the devil— and free those who all their lives were held in slavery by their fear of death. For surely it is not angels he helps, but Abraham's descendants. For this reason he had to be made like his brothers in every way, in order that he might become a merciful and faithful high priest in service to God, and that he might make atonement for the sins of the people. Because he himself suffered when he was tempted, he is able to help those who are being tempted.
(Heb.2:14-18 NIV)

Without the incarnation of God's Word, the rights of sons in connection with the Godhead would not have been given to humans because of the wall of separation that stood between God and us. Christ removed this obstacle by becoming one with humankind. He saved us from sin and brought us to oneness with the eternal Father based on eternal life that he gives to a living soul by faith in his name, through the operation of the Holy Spirit (Jn.10:26-30).

But you don't believe because you are not My sheep. My sheep hear My voice, I know them, and they follow Me. I give them eternal life, and they will never perish—ever! No one will snatch them out of My hand. My Father, who has given them to Me, is greater than all. No one is able to snatch them out of the Father's hand. 30 The Father and I are one.
(HCSB)

In summary, the divine sonship of Christ is due to the oneness he shares with the Godhead because of his pre-existence as the Word of God in the beginning. It was brought to light through incarnation, validated by the Father at his baptism, transfiguration, and through his resurrection.

The ONENESS of GOD

On the other hand, his human sonship is due to incarnation through which he came to oneness with humanity. He is both the Son of Man and the Son of God who brought human race to oneness with the Godhead.

Regarding his Son, who as to his human nature was a descendant of David, and who through the Spirit of holiness was declared with power to be the Son of God by his resurrection from the dead: Jesus Christ our Lord. Through him and for his name's sake, we received grace and apostleship to call people from among all the Gentiles to the obedience that comes from faith.
(Rom.1:3-5 NIV)

Oneness theology asserts that Jesus Christ has a dual nature – human and divine or flesh and spirit but the only difference is that to them, Jesus is the Son of Mary in His human nature while in His divine nature; He is the one God Himself – the Father, Jehovah, the Word and the Holy Spirit. [g]

As the Son of Man, he was born by Mary in Bethlehem Judea, the city of King David as the legitimate heir to his throne, and placed in a manger because there was no room for them at the inn. Later, his parents took him to Galilee where he grew from childhood to adult a Nazarene (Lk.2:1-7, 39-40). As the Son of God, he was given to humanity by the Godhead who sent him to the world, for he pre-existed with him from the beginning as his Word. He obtained the right to govern all things from the Father because of his pre-existence and the great work he accomplished on earth. The duration of his reign on the throne and kingdom of David shall have no end because he lives forever as the Son of God and the Son of Man to establish and uphold his government with justice and righteousness. He is called Wonderful Counselor, Mighty God, Everlasting Father and the Prince of Peace.

DIVINE SONSHIP

For unto us a child is born, unto us a son is given: and the government shall be upon his shoulder: and his name shall be called Wonderful, Counsellor, The mighty God, The everlasting Father, The Prince of Peace. Of the increase of his government and peace there shall be no end, upon the throne of David, and upon his kingdom, to order it, and to establish it with judgment and with justice from henceforth even forever. The zeal of the LORD of hosts will perform this.
(Is. 9:6-7 KJV)

The Lord Jesus is both the "child" (points to his humanity) of the Virgin Mary, and the "Son" (highlights his divinity) of the living God. As a <u>child,</u> he was conceived and born by Mary, from whom he inherited the mortal component and human DNA that constitute part of his being. However, as a <u>Son</u>, he was given (sent) by the Godhead, with whom he subsisted independently as his Word.

The divine essence and DNA in him fused with the human component in an egg cell in Mary's womb as I explained in chapter 3 (under the heading "why Mary played an important role"), to form a living being – an ideal man who was supernaturally conceived and virgin born. His dual nature (human and divine) merged so well that they are indivisible and inseparable. He died on the cross for the sins of humanity because of the human component that formed part of his being, and he rose from death because of the divine essence that constitutes part of his being.

Matthew 27:50 says when Jesus had cried out again in a loud voice, he yielded (gave up) his spirit. John 19:30 informs us that he bowed his head and gave up his spirit after he had tasted the sour wine, and said, "It is finished."

Luke version tells us that he committed his spirit into the hand of the Father before breathing his last (Lk.23:46).

I think the reason is that the divine essence in him could not die, so he has to give it up so he could rescue humanity from eternal condemnation. When he rose from the dead, the mortal component in his body was transformed to immortality by the power of the Holy Spirit, before he ascended bodily to heaven since flesh and blood cannot inherit the kingdom of heaven, nor can mortality inherit immortality.

LESSONS

1. Divine sonship denotes legitimacy, oneness, and union with the Godhead.

2. Christ is called a Son because of the oneness he shares with God and humanity.

3. The sonship of Christ comes in two phases namely, the Son of God and the Son of Man. The former refers to his divine sonship, while the latter refers to his human sonship.

7. To the Jews in Jesus time, the concept of divine sonship denotes equality with the Godhead.

8. Apart from the Godhead, Satan and demonic spirits witness to Jesus' divine sonship.

9. The divine sonship of Jesus was validated at his baptism, transfiguration and through his resurrection.

10. Without the incarnation of Christ, the right of sons in relation to the Godhead would not have been given to humans because of the wall of separation that stood between God and us.

11. Christ destroyed the devil and removed the wall that stood between God and humankind through his death and resurrection.

DIVINE SONSHIP OF CHRISTIAN
STUDY QUESTIONS

1. How is a living soul born again?

2. What are the basic requirements for new birth?

3. How can a person be justified by God?

4. Why is our sonship by adoption?

5. What is the role of the Holy Spirit in new birth?

6. Are we born again by the Holy Spirit or by the word of God?

7. What role do the following factors play in new birth: faith, the blood of Jesus, the word of God and the name of Jesus?

8. Why is God's eternal life infused into the spirit of a person in Christ?

9. Why must a person believe Christ redemptive work and confess his lordship before the individual can be saved?

For as many as are led by the Spirit of God, they are the sons of God. For ye have not received the spirit of bondage again to fear; but ye have received the Spirit of adoption, whereby we cry, Abba, Father. The Spirit itself beareth witness with our spirit, that we are the children of God: And if children, then heirs; heirs of God, and joint-heirs with Christ; if so be that we suffer with him, that we may be also glorified together. (Rom.8:14-17KJV)

Yet to all who received him, to those who believed in his name, he gave the right to become children of God children born not of natural descent, nor of human decision or a husband's will, but born of God. (Jn.1:12-13 NIV)

The ONENESS of GOD

As earlier mentioned, the sonship of a Christian in connection with the Godhead denotes oneness (union) with the eternal Father based on eternal life that is given to the person in Christ Jesus, through the operation of the Holy Spirit who infuses the spirit of the individual with it. This is done in the light of the gospel message that is preached in the name of Jesus the Son of God. A divine activity that is put to effect by the Godhead in Christ, through the ministerial activity of the Holy Spirit also called the Spirit of adoption. This operation brings a person into oneness with the Father in Christ. That is why our divine sonship as believers is not of natural descent, nor of a human decision, but of God through the power of his Spirit in Christ Jesus.

We accept man's testimony, but God's testimony is greater because it is the testimony of God, which he has given about his Son. Anyone who believes in the Son of God has this testimony in his heart. Anyone who does not believe God has made him out to be a liar, because he has not believed the testimony God has given about his Son. And this is the testimony: God has given us eternal life, and this life is in his Son. He who has the Son has life; he who does not have the Son of God does not have life.
(1Jn.5:9-12 NIV)

The Scripture above reveals that the life of the Father that brings a living soul to oneness with him, resides in Jesus of Nazareth. Romans 8:11, says God gives us the life through the Holy Spirit, while 1Corinthians 6:17, declares that we become one in spirit with the Lord when we are joined to him.

DIVINE SONSHIP

The joining with the Lord in spirit occurs when the Holy Spirit infuses (injects) God's eternal life in the spirit man of whoever believes in Christ, and confesses him as Lord and Saviour. Once this is done, the person's spirit is saturated with God's eternal life, which brings the person to oneness with the Father in Christ, through the operation of the Holy Spirit. For without him (Holy Spirit) the life of the Father cannot be given to humans in Christ.

This is how we know that we remain in Him and He in us: He has given to us from His Spirit. And we have seen and we testify that the Father has sent the Son as Savior of the world. Whoever confesses that Jesus is the Son of God —God remains in him and he in God. (1Jn.4:13-15 HCSB)

The divine sonship of a Christian is by adoption, through the ministerial activity of the Holy Spirit who infuses the spirit man of a living soul with the eternal life of the Godhead in Christ Jesus because of Christ atoning sacrifice for the sins of humankind, and his resurrection by which he purchased eternal salvation for humanity. It is through this that he became the author of our salvation and having obtained from the Father the promised Holy Spirit, he poured him out on humans for the salvation of our souls, and the regeneration of our spirit from spiritual death passed on humankind from the beginning through the sin of Adam.

But the gift is not like the trespass. For if the many died by the trespass of the one man, how much more did God's grace and the gift that came by the grace of the one man, Jesus Christ, overflow to the many! Again, the gift of God is not like the result of the one man's sin:

the judgment followed one sin and brought condemnation, but the gift followed many trespasses and brought justification. For if, by the trespass of the one man, death reigned through that one man, how much more will those who receive God's abundant provision of grace and of the gift of righteousness reign in life through the one man, Jesus Christ. Consequently, just as the result of one trespass was condemnation for all men, so also the result of one act of righteousness was justification that brings life for all men. For just as through the disobedience of the one man the many were made sinners, so also through the obedience of the one man the many will be made righteous.
(Rom.5:15-19 NIV)

Nelson's Illustrated Bible Dictionary defines adoption as, "The act of taking voluntarily a child of other parents as one's child." It says the Greek word translated in the New Testament as adoption literally means, "Placing as a son." It adds, "It is a legal term that expresses the process by which a man brings another person into his family, endowing him with the status and privileges of a biological son or daughter." [h]

According to the *International Standard Bible Encyclopaedia*, adoption means, "The legal process by which a man might bring into his family, and endow with the status and privileges of a son, one who was not by nature his son or of his kindred." [I]

Legal process whereby one person receives another into his family and confers upon that person familial privileges and advantages. The "adopter" assumes parental responsibility for the "adoptee." The "adoptee" is thereby considered an actual child, becoming the beneficiary of all the rights, privileges, and responsibilities afforded to all the children of the family. [j]

DIVINE SONSHIP

If adoption means the legal process of granting family rights, privileges and benefits to an individual in order to make the person a recipient of all the advantages given to the children of the family (as shown above), it then implies that our rights as sons of God is bestowed on us through adoption because our divine sonship is by adoption. The Bible declares that we were chosen by God before the creation of the world to be holy and blameless in his sight in love and at the same time predestined to be adopted as his sons through Jesus Christ in order to confer on us the full rights of sons.

Blessed be the God and Father of our Lord Jesus Christ, who has blessed us in Christ with every spiritual blessing in the heavenly places, even as he chose us in him before the foundation of the world, that we should be holy and blameless before him. In love he predestined us for adoption through Jesus Christ, according to the purpose of his will, to the praise of his glorious grace, with which he has blessed us in the Beloved. In him we have redemption through his blood, the forgiveness of our trespasses, according to the riches of his grace, which he lavished upon us, in all wisdom and insight making known to us the mystery of his will, according to his purpose, which he set forth in Christ as a plan for the fullness of time, to unite all things in him, things in heaven and things on earth.
(Eph.1:3-10ESV)

When Christ ascended to heaven, he obtained from the Father, the promised Holy Spirit by whom we are baptized into his body – the church. Hence the name "Spirit of adoption" because through his operation, a living soul is engrafted in Christ by faith.

The ONENESS of GOD

For it is written, "If a man confesses with his mouth that, 'Jesus is Lord,' and believe in his heart that God raised him from the dead, he will be saved. For it is with the heart that a man believes in the sacrificial work of Christ to obtain justification, while with the mouth, confession is made to salvation." (Paraphrased – Romans10:9-10)

This then means that whenever a person believes in their heart that Christ died and rose from the dead for the sins of humankind, the individual will be justified by the Father who imputes his righteousness that is by faith to the person so that he or she can have peace with God in Christ. Now, when the person confesses by the help of the Holy Spirit that Jesus is Lord, the eternal life of the Father will be infused into the spirit of the individual in Christ Jesus. This is done by the power of the Holy Spirit also called the Spirit of Christ for the regeneration of the person's spirit from spiritual death that came on humanity in the beginning through the sin of Adam. This spiritual phenomenon is called "New birth or the baptism by one Spirit into the one body of Christ—the church."

The body is a unit, though it is made up of many parts; and though all its parts are many, they form one body. So it is with Christ. For we were all baptized by one Spirit into one body– whether Jews or Greeks, slave or free – and we were all given the one Spirit to drink. (1Co.12:12-13 NIV)

Therefore, if a person does not have the Spirit of Christ also called the "Spirit of adoption or sonship," he or she does not belong to him according to Scripture (Rom.8:9). Because the life of the Father that brings us to oneness with him resides in Christ but is infused into our spirit through the operation of the Holy Spirit.

DIVINE SONSHIP

By this you know the Spirit of God: Every spirit that confesses that Jesus Christ has come in the flesh is of God, and every spirit that does not confess that Jesus Christ has come in the flesh is not of God. And this is the spirit of the Antichrist, which you have heard was coming, and is now already in the world.

(1Jn.4:2-3 NKJV)

Many in the body of Christ do not agree with the above point of view on the process of salvation. To them, salvation demands repentance from dead works, water baptism in the name of Jesus and Holy Ghost baptism with the evidence of speaking in other tongues. Thus, the "Sinner's Prayer" commonly practiced by majority in the Christendom as the means by which a person is regenerated to enter into the kingdom of God based on Romans 10:9-10 is erroneous because it does not involve water baptism and Holy Spirit baptism.

In his book, *Restoration of the New Testament Church*, Dr. Henry B. Alexander (founder and presiding bishop of the *Shield of Faith Fellowship of Churches, International, Inc.*), explains that for a person to be saved he or she must repent and be baptized both in water and spirit. He writes, "In order for a person to be saved he or she must experience a two-part baptism consisting of both water and spirit. A person who believes the gospel and repents, and subsequently accepts water baptism is forgiven of his sins, and a person who asks for the Holy Ghost in faith will be given it. That person, having repented, been water baptized and then Spirit-filled has then been born into the Kingdom of God." [k]

The ONENESS of GOD

He adds, "Some people falsely teach that a person is born again the instant they pray a prayer, because they fundamentally misunderstand the meaning and context of Romans 10:9-10. Scripture never says that a person is reborn simply by prayer: On the contrary, Jesus insists on "water and Spirit." Scripture ties "rebirth" to both water and Spirit." [l]

Although, he emphasizes that there is nothing negative about the practice of verbal confession, establishing it as the means for new birth is biblically not correct. "While there is nothing negative in or about the practice of verbal confession, yet it *alone* can never be construed as the means by which a person enters into the Kingdom of God." [m]

In effect, a closer look at Romans10:8-10 reveals that the "word of faith," "confession," and "believe" play distinct roles in the process of salvation. The word of faith produces the faith we need to please God (Heb.11:6), believing that God raised Jesus from death causes him to impute his righteousness that is by faith to us (Rom.4:22-25). Confessing the lordship of Jesus makes God to infuse our spirit with his life for rebirth. To say that salvation comes by merely verbalizing the "Sinner's Prayer" without faith in Christ atoning sacrifice that comes from hearing the gospel message, repentance from dead works and openly confessing Jesus as Lord and Savior is biblically incorrect.

In conclusion, we are born again or given a newness of life by the Godhead in Christ Jesus his Son, through the operation of the Holy Spirit. A spiritual activity that is done in the light of the word of truth, which is the gospel massage preached in the name of Jesus Christ.

DIVINE SONSHIP

The Bible declares that he chose to give us birth through the word of truth that we might be a kind of firstfruits of all he created (Jas.1:18). Without the help or divine operation of the Holy Spirit, nobody can ever admit and confess that Jesus is Lord, which are the basic requirements for the salvation of a living soul (1Co.12:3).

The eternal life of the Godhead that resides in Christ cannot be infused into the spirit man of a living soul by the Holy Spirit unless the individual acknowledges the atoning sacrificial work of Christ on the cross of Calvary and confesses his lordship. "For in Christ Jesus you are all sons of God, through faith." (Gal.3:21ESV)

LESSONS

1. A person is born again when God's eternal life is infused into his or her spirit man through the operation of the Holy Spirit, at the hearing of the word of faith that is preached in Jesus name.

2. It is required that a living soul believes Christ atoning sacrificial work and confesses his lordship, for with the heart one believes and is justified, while with the mouth confession is made to salvation.

3. A person is justified by the Godhead who imputes his righteousness by faith on him or her when the individual accepts and believes that Christ died for the sins of humankind, and rose for our justification.

4. Our sonship is by adoption because the right of sons in relation to the Godhead is bestowed on us through it.

5. The Holy Spirit convicts us of sins, (b) he convinces us of eternal judgement and the need to accept Christ atoning sacrifice,

(c) he helps us to believe and confess the lordship of Christ, (d) he infuses our spirit man with the eternal life of God.

6. We are regenerated by the word of God through the operation of the Holy Spirit.

7. Ephesians 3:17, says Christ dwells in our hearts through faith, while Hebrew11:6 declares that none can please God without faith. (b) The blood of Jesus washes our sins and iniquities. (c) The word of God generates the faith we need to please God. (d) The Holy Spirit uses the blood, the word, and faith to regenerate a living soul in Christ. (e) Jesus is the only name given among men for salvation.

8. God's eternal life is infused into the spirit man of a person for a newness of life in Christ Jesus.

9. Believing in Christ's redemptive work causes a person to obtain God's righteousness and be at peace with him, while confessing Christ lordship makes the Holy Spirit to infuse the person's spirit with God's eternal life.

10. The Bible declares that there is no other name given to humans under heaven for the salvation of their souls except the name of Jesus (Acts4:12).

SUPERIORITY
OF THE SONSHIP OF JESUS

STUDY QUESTIONS

1. Why is Jesus divine sonship superior to that of other people?

2. What is the basis for its superiority?

3. How significant is the superiority of his sonship to the others?

DIVINE SONSHIP

The sonship of Christ in connection with the Godhead is superior to that of Adam, Israel and Christian because of his pre-existence with the Father in the beginning (Micah5:2, Lk.1:31-32, Heb.7:3).

SONSHIP OF ADAM: Adam is declared the son of God in Luke3:38, because he was created in the image and likeness of God in the beginning, which then made him one with the Godhead. The sonship of Adam in connection with the Godhead is due to his creation in the image and likeness of God (Gen.1:26-27).

SONSHIP OF ISRAEL: (Ex.4:22-23) the sonship of Israel in relation to the Godhead is by adoption, because God chose them from among all the nations of the world, to be his peculiar people—holy and sanctified. This brought them into oneness with the Godhead in accordance with his predetermined will and counsel, which he programmed before the world began. He made himself their God and Father, he revealed his name, will, purpose, and ways to them (Gen.17:7, Ps.135:4, Rom.9:4, 5, 10-16, 11:28-29).

SONSHIP OF CHRISTIAN: (Jn.1:12-13, Rom.1:12-13, 8:15-17) the sonship of a Christian in connection with the Godhead is by adoption through the operation of the Holy Spirit, who is also called the Spirit of adoption or the spirit of Christ. He infuses the spirit man of a living soul with the eternal life of God by faith and revelation knowledge of the word of truth, for a newness of life in Christ Jesus the author of our salvation (Gal.4:4-7, Eph.1-6).

In summary, the sonship of Jesus Christ as regards to the Godhead is superior to that of Adam, Israel, and Christian because he pre-existed with the Father from the beginning as his Word. In addition, he is one of the two constituent elements that make up the eternal power of God.

LESSONS

Jesus sonship is superior to that of other people because he is one with the Godhead in essence, and he pre-existed with him in the beginning as his Word. All things were created through him according to Scripture, which also made him head over every existing thing.

CHAPTER 11

ELOHIM

STUDY QUESTIONS

1. What is the meaning of the word Elohim?

2. How does it highlight the plurality within the Godhead?

3. Whom was God talking to when he said, "Let us…"

4. How was the fullness of God revealed in the beginning?

5. What is the difference between "God, his Word and Spirit," and "God the Father, Jesus the Son, and the Holy Spirit?"

6. What is the difference between "God the Father, God the Son and God the Holy Spirit," and "God the Father, Jesus the Son of God, and the Holy Spirit?"

The *International Standard Bible Encyclopedia – Revised Edition* says the use of the plural form of Elohim with singular meaning is not unique to Israel. It states that similar forms occur in pre-Israelite Babylonian and Canaanite texts in which a worshiper wishes to exalt a particular god above others.

The ONENESS of GOD

"This form has been called the "plural of majesty" or the "intensive plural" because it implies that all the fulness of deity is concentrated in the one god. 'Elohim's being the most common word for God in the OT thus conveys this idea." [a]

Elohim is the plural form of El, but it is usually translated in the singular. Some scholars have held that the plural represents an intensified form for the supreme God; others believe it describes the supreme God and His heavenly court of created beings. Still others hold that the plural form refers to the triune God of Gen 1:1-3, who works through Word and Spirit in the creation of the world. All agree that the plural form Elohim does convey the sense of the one supreme being who is the only true God. [b]

From the above different points of view, we understand that the word "Elohim" is a grammatically singular or plural noun for god or gods. Nonetheless, when referring to the God of Israel, it is grammatically singular in meaning but plural in use. *Wikipedia encyclopedia* puts it this way, "In the Hebrew Bible Elohim, when meaning the God of Israel, is mostly grammatically singular. Even in Genesis 1:26 "Then God said (singular verb), 'Let us make (plural verb) man in our image, after our likeness'." Elohim is singular." [c]

Rev. Bernard mentions that the use of the plural word Elohim indicates God's greatness or his multitude attribute; but insists it does not imply a plurality of persons or personalities. In addition, he says, "The Bible itself reveals that the only way to understand the plural form of Elohim is that it expresses God's majesty and not a plurality in the Godhead." [d]

ELOHIM

According to *Smith's Bible Dictionary*, the etymology of the word is uncertain but the primary idea is generally agreed to be that of strength, power of effect and it properly describes God in that character in which he is exhibited to all men in his works as the creator, sustainer and supreme governor of the world. It also says the plural form of the word has given rise to much discussion and the fanciful idea that it referred to the trinity of person in the Godhead hardly finds now a supporter among scholars. [e]

The use of the word Elohim when meaning the God of Israel highlights the plurality within the Godhead as in the Scriptures below.

And God [Elohim] said, Let us make man in our image, after our likeness: and let them have dominion over the fish of the sea, and over the fowl of the air, and over the cattle, and over all the earth, and over every creeping thing that creepeth upon the earth. So God [Elohim] created man in his own image, in the image of God [Elohim] created he him; male and female created he them.
(Gen.1:26-27 KJV)

Then the Lord God said, "Behold, the man has become like one of Us, knowing good and evil; and now, lest he stretch out his hand, and take also from the tree of life, and eat, and live forever.
(Gen. 3:22 NASB)

In his book, *The 7 Habits of Highly Effective People*, author Stephen R. Covey describes the concept of interdependence as the paradigm of we – we can do it; we can cooperate; we can combine our talents and abilities and create something greater together. He explains that interdependent people combine their own efforts with the efforts of others to achieve their greatest success.

To illustrate his point, he writes, "If I am physically interdependent, I am self-reliant and capable, but I also realize that you and I working together can accomplish far more than, even at my best, I could accomplish alone." [f]

With this and the above Scriptures in mind, I think it is necessary to ask ourselves a very important question as to whom God was talking when he said, "Let us make man in our likeness or the man has become like one of us, knowing good and evil" (which highlights the concept of interdependence). Although, the Bible remains silent about whom God was speaking to, it is evident from Scripture that no angelic being was involved in the work of creation.

Oneness theology affirms that the Jews traditionally interpreted this passage to mean God talked to the angels at creation. However, it does not imply that they actually took part in creation says the doctrine, except that God informed them of his plans and solicited their comments out of courtesy and respect. [g]

Rev. Bernard says that Genesis 1:26 cannot mean a plurality in the Godhead, for that would contradict the rest of Scripture. Therefore, he offered the following explanations for the passage. "(1) The Jews and many Christians see this as a reference to the angels. Many other Christians see it as (2) a description of God counseling with His own will, (3) a majesty or literary plural, (4) a pronoun simply agreeing with the noun Elohim, or (5) a prophetic reference to the future manifestation of the Son of God." [h]

ELOHIM

From our earlier note on the nature of God, we understood that the Lord God is indivisibly one in essence, and that his being is made up of his eternal power and divine nature. We also discover that his eternal power comprises his Word and Spirit in the beginning. Now, if they were both directly involved in God's creation activities as revealed in the Bible (Ps.33:6), it stands to reason that the Godhead was addressing his Word and Spirit when he said, "Let us make man in Our likeness (Gen.1:26)" or "the man has become like one of Us, knowing good and evil (Gen.3:22)." The reason is that they both subsisted in him as individual beings in the beginning. And since the beginning of God's works commenced before the creation of man, I believe the Godhead addressed his Word and Spirit as distinct beings in Genesis1:26.

To Bernard, any interpretation of Genesis1:26 that permit the existence of more than one person of God runs into severe difficulties since Isaiah 44:24 says the Lord created the heavens alone and created the earth by Himself. [i] It is true God made all things by himself. However, he did it through his Word and Spirit (Ps.33:6).

The God of the Bible is indivisibly one eternal true God who granted his eternal power the right to subsist independently in eternity past, and it subsisted in him as his Word and Spirit, though with one essence. That is to say, though they exist distinctly in the Godhead, they are not different from him in essence because they make up his eternal power, which is the first constituent of God. The Word and Spirit of God are merely an extension of his being.

The ONENESS of GOD

So, for the Bible to say in Isaiah 44:24 that God created the heavens alone and the earth by himself is a proof that his Word and Spirit whom he used in creating all things (Ps.33:6, Jn.1:3, Col.1:16), are indivisibly and inseparably one with him, even though they subsist as individual beings. Below are some proof texts to support this idea:

And the LORD God [Elohim] said, "The man has now become like one of us, knowing good and evil. He must not be allowed to reach out his hand and take also from the tree of life and eat, and live forever.
(Gen.3:22 NIV)

... Behold, they are one people, and they have all one language, and this is only the beginning of what they will do. And nothing that they propose to do will now be impossible for them. Come, let us go down and there confuse their language so that they may not understand one another's speech.
(Gen.11:6-7 ESV)

Then I heard the voice of the Lord, saying, "Whom shall I send, and who will go for Us?" Then I said, "Here am I. Send me!"
(Is.6:8 NASB)

Thus, paraphrasing the book of Genesis 1:26-27, would read as follow:

Then God [Elohim] said, [to His eternal power that subsisted in him as his Word and Spirit]. "Let us make man in our image, in our likeness, and let them rule over the fish of the sea and the birds of the air, over the livestock, over all the earth, and over all the creatures that move along the ground." So God [Elohim] created man in his own image, in the image of God [Elohim] he created him; male and female he created them.

ELOHIM

This then means that the Godhead existed in the beginning as "God, his Word and Spirit." However, because of the incarnation of his Word, he now exists as "Father, Son and Spirit." The existence of the one and only true God as Father, Son and Spirit does not signify three separates Gods as some Trinitarians claim for that would imply Tritheism, neither does it mean different manifestations, roles, titles, attributes or functions as Modalists claim for that also would mean Modalism. Nonetheless, the truth lies in-between these two lines of arguments and views because God is intrinsically one in essence but granted his Word and Spirit the right to subsist individually in him, meaning there is one God in three distinct beings because of Christ. The plurality or threeness in the Godhead is not in essence or nature, will, purpose etc. but in being. That is why the Father is not the Son; the Son is not the Holy Spirit, and the Holy Spirit is neither the Father nor the Son. They all have individuality with one essence – i.e. though God is one in nature, he is three in being.

The grace of the Lord Jesus Christ, and the love of God, and the fellowship of the Holy Spirit, be with you all.
(2Co.13:14NASB)

How God anointed Jesus of Nazareth with the Holy Spirit and with power, who went about doing good and healing all who were oppressed by the devil, for God was with Him.
(Acts 10:38 NKJV)

Then Jesus came to them and said, "All authority in heaven and on earth has been given to me. Therefore go and make disciples of all nations, baptizing them in the name of the Father and of the Son and of the Holy Spirit."
(Matt.28:18-20 NIV)

The ONENESS of GOD

Consequently, we have "God the Father, Jesus the Son, and the Holy Spirit" because of his eternal love and plan for humanity, which he brought to light in the person of Jesus Christ.2Timothy1:9-10 says that God saved and called us to a holy life, not according to our works but because of his own purpose, and grace that was given us in Christ Jesus before the world began; but it has now be revealed through the appearing of our Saviour Jesus Christ. Who abolished death, and brought life and immortality to light through the gospel. Without the incarnation of God's Word, the fatherhood of God, sonship of Christ, and the person of the Holy Spirit being the highest order in the self-revelation of the one and only true eternal God would not have been possible.

Do not be ashamed then of testifying to our Lord, nor of me his prisoner, but share in suffering for the gospel in the power of God, who saved us and called us with a holy calling, not in virtue of our works but in virtue of his own purpose and the grace which he gave us in Christ Jesus ages ago, and now has manifested through the appearing of our Savior Christ Jesus, who abolished death and brought life and immortality to light through the gospel.
(2 Tim.1:8-11RSV)

And to make plain to everyone the administration of this mystery, which for ages past was kept hidden in God, who created all things. His intent was that now, through the church, the manifold wisdom of God should be made known to the rulers and authorities in the heavenly realms, according to his eternal purpose which he accomplished in Christ Jesus our Lord.
(Eph.3:9-11 NIV)

ELOHIM

Hence, we see the Godhead as the chief operator and visionary, putting all his work to effect in the person of Jesus Christ who is the administrator of all divine activities, through the power of the Holy Spirit being the executor of all divine counsels and purposes as in the Scripture below.

Now there are <u>varieties of gifts,</u> but <u>the same Spirit</u>; and there are <u>varieties of service</u>, but <u>the same Lord</u>; and there are <u>varieties of activities,</u> but <u>it is the same God</u> who empowers them all in everyone. (1Co.12:4-6 ESV)

This verse of the Bible reveals the eternal existence, distinctiveness, division of labor, unity of purpose, hierarchy within the Godhead who existed as "God, his Word and Spirit" in the beginning. However, for the sake of humanity, he now exists as "God the Father, Jesus the Son and the Holy Spirit" because of Christ who is the exact representation of the Deity to humankind. For this reason, we serve and worship the Father as believers in Christ, through the help and power of the Holy Spirit. So that in all things, the Son of God, Jesus of Nazareth, might be honored and glorified according to the will and predetermined counsel of the Father.

LESSONS

1. When referring to the God of Israel, Elohim is grammatically singular in meaning but plural in use.

2. Elohim highlights the plurality within the Godhead because it reveals the fact that though God is one in essence; he exists in three distinct divine persons.

The ONENESS of GOD

3. God was addressing both his Word and Spirit when he said, "Let us…" Since both of them subsisted in him as distinct divine beings in the beginning.

4. The Word and Spirit of God were both involved in the work of creation.

5. The Godhead existed in the beginning as God, his Word and Spirit but due to the incarnation of his Word, he now exists as God the Father, Jesus the Son and the Holy Spirit.

6. The Godhead is the chief operator and visionary of all divine activities; Jesus Christ is the administrator, while the Holy Spirit is the sole executor of all divine counsels and purposes.

7. As Christians, we serve and worship the Godhead in Christ Jesus, through the help and power of the Holy Spirit.

CHAPTER 12

THE TRINITY

STUDY QUESTIONS

1. What is the doctrine of the trinity all about?

2. Why is it characterized by a plurality of views and formulations?

3. How was it developed?

4. Why are people confused about the doctrine?

5. How is the trinity not tritheism?

6. Why is the credibility of the doctrine often question by many?

7. Why do some people consider the doctrine as heresy or anti-biblical?

8. Should the word "trinity" be used to explain God?

9. If yes, how should it be employed?

The word "trinity" is not found in the Bible, but some theologians used it to convey the biblical teaching that God is not only one in nature but also three in persons. It states that each person in the Godhead is coequal and coeternal but differs in function. *Holman Illustrated Bible Dictionary* refers to the word as a theological term used to define God as an undivided unity expressed in the threefold nature of God the Father, God the Son, and God the Holy Spirit. [a]

The ONENESS of GOD

According to *Mathew Easton*, the propositions involved in the doctrine are: (1) God is one, and there is but one God (Deut 6:4). (2) The Father is a distinct divine Person, distinct from the Son and the Holy Spirit. (3) Jesus Christ was truly God, and yet was a Person distinct from the Father and the Holy Spirit. (4) The Holy Spirit is also a distinct divine Person." [b]

We are not using Biblical language when we define what is expressed by it as the doctrine that there is one only and true God, but in the unity of the Godhead there are three coeternal and coequal Persons, the same in substance but distinct in subsistence." [c]

In his book, *The Holy Spirit*, Evangelist Billy Graham writes, "The Holy Spirit is one with the Father and the Son. If the Father is God, and Jesus is God, then the Holy Spirit is also God." He continues, "The chief problem connected with the doctrine of the Trinity concerns Christianity's claim to be also monotheistic. It rejects polytheism, the belief in more than one God. The answer is that Trinitarianism preserves the unity of the Godhead, and at the same time it acknowledges that there are three persons in that Godhead which is still of one essence. God is one, but that oneness is not simple—it is complex." [d]

Some use the word to mean the unity of three persons in one God – Father, Son and Holy Spirit. Others use it to mean there is but one God; within the one God are three personalities and wills. A number of people hold that in God are three distinctions of natures, persons and wills.

THE TRINITY

Dake writes, "What we mean by Divine Trinity is that there are three separate and distinct persons in the Godhead, each one having his own personal spirit body, personal soul and personal spirit in the same sense each human being, angel or any other being has his own body, soul and spirit. We mean by body, whether a spirit body or flesh body, the house for the indwelling of the personal soul and spirit. The soul is that which feels and the spirit is that which knows." [e]

The *International Standard Bible Encyclopedia* informs us that the doctrine can be spoken of as Biblical only on the principle that the sense of Scripture is Scripture and the definition of a Biblical doctrine in such un-Biblical language can be justified only on the principle that it is better to preserve the truth of Scripture than the words of Scripture. [f]

The doctrine remains one of the most controversial subjects in the Christendom. I think one of the main reasons it is characterized by a plurality of views, opinions, and interpretations is because the "how" of the doctrine has not been fully explained since the beginning of the history of the church as some have done with the "fact" of it that the Scripture presents. We understand from the Bible that the Father is not the Son, the Son is not the Holy Spirit, and neither is the Holy Spirit the Father nor the Son. These are facts that Scriptures clearly point out from the book of Genesis to Revelation to support this notion. Nevertheless, the "how" of the distinction of beings in the Godhead remains a mystery since the Bible does not clearly reveal it like it did with the "fact." For this reason, the subject has become one of much debate among Christians and non-Christians.

The ONENESS of GOD

In an attempt to answer the various questions people ask about the "how" of the doctrine, many views, opinions, and interpretations have been put forward by men and women in the body of Christ.

In his annotated reference Bible, Dake listed what he called eighteen (18) fallacies about the Trinity. It includes the following:

1. That there is only one person or one being called God

2. That there is a difference in meaning of three human persons and three divine persons

3. That the terms Father, Son, and Holy Ghost refer to three manifestations of one person or one being

4. That the Father is the only person who is divine; the Son was created by the Father; and the Holy Ghost was created by the Son (Arianism)

5. That God consists of three persons in one person or three beings in one being

6. That the Father, Son, and Holy Ghost are essential parts of one being, just as man is made up of body, soul, and spirit

7. That God is a complex person and so it is folly to seek to explain the Trinity

8. That the Trinity is beyond human comprehension and bewilders the most learned

9. That the Trinity is not an O.T revelation

10. That God has no body, bodily parts, or passions like human beings – nothing of a bodily nature

11. That God is invisible reality and cannot be seen by natural eyes

THE TRINITY

12. That God is a universal mind, conscience, love, goodness, and power filling all space and matter

13. That there is nothing on earth to resemble him

14. That God cannot be comprehended by the senses but by the soul, for He is above sensuous perceptions

15. The image of God consists only of moral and spiritual likeness

16. That all statements of God having a body with bodily parts are mere figures of speech conveying some idea of God to man

17. That Jesus Christ is the Father, Son, and Holy Ghost

18. That Jesus is the one God and Jehovah of the O.T

He states that all such statements are unscriptural in the extreme and are contradicted by thousands of plain passages about God. He asks, "Why would God tell us that all invisible things are <u>clearly seen</u> by visible things on earth, even to His eternal power and Godhead (Rom.1:20), if He is incomprehensible; if there is nothing on earth to resemble Him; if He is a bodiless being; if He is three beings in one being; if His image is only moral and spiritual; if descriptions of His body and bodily parts are not true and real; and if He is an invisible nothingness floating in nowhere? If this is what God is why did He not say this instead of what he did say? Is it possible that He does not speak to us in plain human language? Or, is it possible that the church and false religions are in error and that God does mean what he says about Himself? Who gave man the right to change the Bible from a literal to an imaginative meaning? If statements about God are mere figures of speech trying to convey some idea of Him, what ideas do they convey? That He does not have a body with bodily parts, or that He does? That He is less real than His creations, or that He is as real?

The ONENESS of GOD

It would be unlike God to say over 20,000 things about Himself if He did not have a personal body, soul and spirit as stated." [g]

The doctrine of the Trinity lies in Scripture in solution; when it is crystallized from its solvent it does not cease to be Scriptural, but only comes into clearer view. Or, to speak without figure, the doctrine of the Trinity is given to us in Scripture, not in formulated definition, but in fragmentary allusions; when we assemble the disjecta membra into their organic unity, we are not passing from Scripture, but entering more thoroughly into the meaning of Scripture. [h]

For this reason, *Holman Illustrated Bible Dictionary* says it is considered as a divine mystery beyond human comprehension to be reflected upon only through Scriptural revelation. It adds that the Trinity is a biblical concept that expresses the dynamic character of God, not a Greek idea pressed into Scripture from philosophical or religious speculation. While the term "trinity" does not appear in Scripture, the Trinitarian structure appears throughout the NT to affirm that God Himself is manifested through Jesus Christ by means of the Spirit. [I]

Likewise, David Stern says the word "trinity" does not appear in the New Testament; but was developed later by theologians trying to express profundities, which God has revealed, about himself. According to him, the New Testament does not teach tritheism, which is belief in three gods; it does not teach unitarianism, which denies the divinity of Yeshua the Son and of the Holy Spirit. Neither does it teach modalism, which says that God appears sometimes as the Father, sometimes as the Son and sometimes as the Holy Spirit, like an actor changing masks. [j]

THE TRINITY

Some believe that though the Deity is indivisibly one in essence, he exists in three separates persons, as God the Father, God the Son and God the Holy Spirit. Others believe the Father, Son and Holy Spirit are merely different manifestations, roles and functions of the one God and that it does not signify distinctions of persons. Still some affirm that Christ and the Holy Spirit pre-existed as the Word and Spirit of God, and that they both subsisted in the Godhead from the beginning as distinct divine beings. Quite a few others believe that God is one and only, there is none equal to him and that Christ and the Holy Spirit are less superior to him.

A proper biblical view of the Trinity balances the concepts of unity and distinctiveness. Two errors that appear in the history of the consideration of the doctrine are tritheism and unitarianism. In tritheism error is made in emphasizing the distinctiveness of the Godhead to the point that the Trinity is seen as three separate Gods, or a Christian polytheism. On the other hand, unitarianism excludes the concept of distinctiveness while focusing solely on the aspect of God the Father. In this way Christ and the Holy Spirit are placed in lower categories and made less than divine. Both errors compromise the effectiveness and contribution of the activity of God in redemptive history. [ᵏ]

While Trinitarians say there are three persons in one God, and that God is the Holy Trinity, Oneness asserts there is one God with no plurality of persons, but that he does have a plurality of manifestations, roles, titles, attributes or relationships to man. The first claim the Father, Son and Holy Spirit are the three persons in the Godhead and that they are co-equal, co-eternal and of one essence with God the Father as the head of the Trinity.

The ONENESS of GOD

Jesus Christ is the incarnation of God the Son and he is not the Father or the Holy Spirit. The later holds that Father, Son and Holy Spirit are different designations for the one God and that God is both the Father and the Holy Spirit, while the Son is God manifest in flesh. To them, the term Son refers to the incarnation, and never to deity apart from humanity. Jesus Christ is the incarnation of the fullness of God, and in his deity, he is both the Father and the Holy Spirit. [l]

In his response to Christianity Today article, "Apologetics Journal Criticizes Jakes" *Bishop T.D Jakes* said that many things could be said about the Son that cannot be said about the Father. "The Son was born of a virgin; the Father created the virgin from whom he was born. The Son slept (Luke 8:23), but the Father never sleeps (Ps. 121:3-5). The Son took on the likeness of sinful flesh (Romans 8:3), but God is a spirit (John 4:24). Likewise, several characteristics are distinctive to the Holy Spirit (John 16:13) … In spite of all the distinctives, God is one in his essence. Though no human illustration perfectly fits the Divine, it is similar to ice, water, and steam: three separate forms, yet all H2O. Each element can co-exist, each has distinguishing characteristics and functions, but all have sameness." [m]

In conclusion, I would say there is only one true God, the maker of heaven and earth. He existed in the beginning as God, his Word and Spirit before sending his Word to rescue human souls from death. A mission he accomplished on the cross by offering himself as sin offering in favor of humanity. Having accomplished an excellent work on earth, he ascended to heaven as a Son and sat at the right hand of the throne of God to mediate for humankind.

THE TRINITY

This in turn caused a change in the existence of the Deity from "God, his Word, and Spirit" to "God, his Son – Jesus Christ, and his Spirit called the Holy Spirit." This change occurred because of Christ and God's eternal love for humanity.

The "Trinity" should rather be employed to express the existence of the one and only true God in three distinct persons, as God the Father, Jesus Christ his Son, and the Holy Spirit instead of God the Father, God the Son and God the Holy Spirit. My reason is that the latter entails tritheism, which is a belief in three gods.

According to the foreknowledge of God the Father, by the sanctifying work of the Spirit, that you may obey Jesus Christ and be sprinkled with His blood: May grace and peace be yours in fullest measure.
(1 Pet.1:2 NASB)

And I will pray the Father, and he shall give you another Comforter, that he may abide with you forever; Even the Spirit of truth; whom the world cannot receive, because it seeth him not, neither knoweth him: but ye know him; for he dwelleth with you, and shall be in you. But the Comforter, which is the Holy Ghost, whom the Father will send in my name, he shall teach you all things, and bring all things to your remembrance, whatsoever I have said unto you.
(Jn.14:16-17, 26 KJV)

In point of fact, the doctrine of the Trinity is purely a revealed doctrine. That is to say, it embodies a truth which has never been discovered, and is indiscoverable, by natural reason. With all his searching, man has not been able to find out for himself the deepest things of God. Accordingly, ethnic thought has never attained a Trinitarian conception of God, nor does any ethnic religion present in its representations of the divine being any analogy to the doctrine of the Trinity. [n]

The ONENESS of GOD

As the doctrine of the Trinity is indiscoverable by reason, so it is incapable of proof from reason. There are no analogies to it in Nature, not even in the spiritual nature of man, who is made in the image of God. In His trinitarian mode of being, God is unique; and, as there is nothing in the universe like Him in this respect, so there is nothing which can help us to comprehend Him. Many attempts have, nevertheless, been made to construct a rational proof of the Trinity of the God head. Among these there are two which are particularly attractive, and have therefore been put forward again and again by speculative thinkers through all the Christian ages. These are derived from the implications, in the one case, of self-consciousness; in the other, of love. Both self-consciousness and love, it is said, demand for their very existence an object over against which the self stands as subject. If we conceive of God as self-conscious and loving, therefore, we cannot help conceiving of Him as embracing in His unity some form of plurality. From this general position both arguments have been elaborated, however, by various thinkers in very varied forms. [°]

LESSONS

1. The word "trinity" is not found in the Bible, but theologians developed it to express the mystery God revealed about himself in the Bible.

2. The doctrine is characterized by a plurality of views, opinions, and interpretations because the "how" of it transcends human comprehension.

3. People are confused about the doctrine because of the diverse opinions and believe many have about it.

THE TRINITY

4. Many people question the credibility of the doctrine because some believe God is one and exclude the concept of distinctiveness, while others focus on the existence of God in three separates persons.

5. Many consider the doctrine as anti-biblical because the word "trinity" is not found in the Bible. They think such word should not be used to express the nature of the Godhead.

6. The word trinity should be employ to express the existence of the Godhead as God the Father, Jesus his Son and the Holy Spirit, rather than God the Father, God the Son, and God the Holy Spirit.

CHAPTER 13

ONENESS OF GOD

According to the Bible, the creator of heaven and earth is intrinsically one eternal Lord, whose being is made up of his eternal power and divine nature. He made all things for his own pleasure in accordance with his will and counsel. None is equal to him in heaven, on earth or beneath the earth. He lives, reigns and sustains all things by his great power that enables him to keep all things under control from one generation to another. Because of his eternal plan and purpose that he programmed before the world began to be accomplished in Christ, he caused his eternal power to subsist in him as individual being, and it subsisted as his Word and Spirit.

At the appointed time, he sent his Word to die for the sins of humanity. The Word became flesh, died on the cross, rose from the dead and ascended bodily to the right hand throne of God. There he obtained the Holy Spirit from the Father, who also made him both Lord and Christ.

The ONENESS of GOD

His bodily presence in the throne room of heaven caused a change in the existence of the one eternal God from – God, his Word and Spirit to – God the Father, Jesus his Son and the Holy Spirit. This means that the Father, Son and Spirit in the Godhead does not signify three separates gods, neither does it indicates mere manifestations, titles, roles or functions. It rather signifies the highest level of self-revelation of the one and only true eternal God (the maker of heaven and earth) to humanity.

In his note on *the doctrine of the absolute oneness of God*, Dr. Alexander explains, "From Genesis to Revelation, the Word of God is emphatic about the fact that there is only one God. Although He has revealed Himself as Father in creation, Son in the redemption of mankind, and Holy Ghost as He indwells the believer, He is utterly and absolutely One God." [a]

While writing on the primary manifestations of God through human history, he further explains that God first existed as an eternal Spirit usually called "the Father" who fashioned the creation in his mind…. At the appointed time He was born into "normal" human flesh…. In the days of human flesh He lived as an example, died as the sacrifice, and rose again from the dead…. When the day of Pentecost arrived, this same One God came back again, this time as the Holy Spirit which would inhabit the hearts of those who would receive Him…. When this age ends in the Rapture of the church, Jesus will be with His Bride in Heaven until the time for the Battle of Armageddon…. At that time He will return to earth again in the same body that He carried 2000 years ago.

ONENESS OF GOD

He will rule the nations as the Messiah of Israel, and the King of Kings – in that same physical body. When the millennium is finished He will sit on the throne of Judgment in the same physical body until the Judgment is completed. Then both He and the church will return to the eternal future where the "Sonship" will be done away with, and God will be all in all. [b]

To him, Jesus is the Father as to his divinity, the Son as to his Humanity and the Holy Spirit as to his eternal substance, activity and source of being. Thus, Father, Son, and Holy Spirit are merely three offices and titles of relationship and activity. [c]

The main problem I have with this absolute oneness view of the Godhead is that it takes one aspect of the truth revealed about God in the Bible and pushes it to an unbalance extreme.

The Bible clearly reveals that Jesus is not the Father, Son, and Holy Spirit. The Father is God; Jesus is both God and man because he is one with the Godhead, and humanity in essence. The Holy Spirit is also a distinct being that is one with the Godhead in essence. That is to say, though there is one God in essence, he exists in three separates beings (persons) as the Father, Son, and Spirit because of Christ and his eternal love for humankind. Christ in who dwells God's Word and Spirit in bodily form is an extension of God.

In conclusion, the Godhead is one eternal Spirit whose power and divine nature constitute the fullness of his being in eternity past. His works began in eternity when he – the one true God – allowed his eternal power to subsist in him as the "Word" and "Spirit."

The ONENESS of GOD

The incarnation, death, resurrection and ascension of his Word to heaven as "Jesus the Son of God" changed the state of the Godhead to "Father, Son and Holy Spirit." Thus, the Father, Son, and Spirit are not merely different functions that the one true God assumed at diverse times in history neither is it the different modes through which Jesus manifested to humanity. Instead, it is the highest level of self-revelation of the one God who now exists simultaneously as Father, Son, and Holy Spirit because of the church – the body and bride of Christ. The Father, Son, and Spirit exist simultaneously as one in essence but distinct in being.

CHAPTER 14

FULLNESS OF GOD

The Bible declares in Colossians 2:9 that in Christ dwells all the fullness of the Godhead in bodily form. Several interpretations have been made on this passage since the beginning of church history. Some say the fullness of the Godhead dwells in Christ because he is all that make up the Deity. That is to say, the Father, Son, and Spirit formed the one person called Christ. Others believe God has no body as a spirit being, and the only body he prepared for himself to dwell in is that of Christ. A few believe the reason the fullness of the Godhead dwells in Christ is that he is God the Father.

For in Christ all the fullness of the Deity lives in bodily form. *(NIV)*

About the passage, Rev. Bernard writes, "We understand this to mean all of God – all His attributes, power, and character – is in Jesus. Father, Son, Holy Ghost, Jehovah, Word, and so on are all in Jesus." [a] That is to say, to the oneness believers, the fullness of the Godhead dwells in Jesus Christ because he is the Father, Son, Spirit, Word, Jehovah etc.

The ONENESS of GOD

As I mentioned in the beginning of this book, the fullness of God has to do with the eternal constituent of his being. Under the heading, "Nature of God" we discover that though God has many attributes, his everlasting power and divine nature are the two fundamental constituents of his being. In addition, we saw that these two intrinsic eternal attributes of God makes up the fullness of his being in eternity past.

In chapter two, we also learned that the beginning (this stands for when God's works started) commenced when God caused his eternal power to subsist as individual being, and it subsisted in him as his Word and Spirit. For this reason, Scripture declares in John 1:1 that in the beginning was the Word because the beginning of God's activities started with him. Consequently, the fullness of God's eternal being in the beginning consists of his Word, Spirit, and divine nature.

Paraphrasing John 1:1 would read as follow:

In the beginning [when God's works started in eternity past] was the Word, and the Word was with God [as a distinct divine being from the moment he transitioned from merely being part of the constituents of God's eternal power to independent subsistent], and the Word was God [because he is one with the Godhead in essence].

After the incarnation, death, resurrection and bodily ascension of God's Word to heaven, the Bible declared in Acts 2:33 that he obtained the Holy Spirit from the Father. From that moment, the Holy Spirit moved from the Father and dwelt in Christ, which means that in the glorified body of Jesus lives the Word and Spirit of God that constitute God's eternal power.

FULLNESS OF GOD

In addition, God's Word and Spirit are one with the Godhead in essence, even though they both reside in Christ as a unified entity, which then implies that in Christ live the Word, Spirit and the divine nature of God. These three eternal components constitute the fullness of God in the beginning, and they all dwell in Christ the head of the church. For better understanding, I would say that Christ is an extension of the Godhead and the replicate of all that makes him up.

This means that Christ is not the Father, Son and Spirit as oneness believer's claim. It simply means that everything that makes up the Godhead are in him so that whoever sees him, sees the Father because he is the exact representation of his invisible being to humanity (Col.1:15, Heb.1:3). John14:8-11 recounts Jesus' response when Philip asked him to show them the Father. In verses 9 and 10, the Lord asked, "Don't you know me, Philip even after I have been among you such a long time? Anyone who has seen me has seen the Father. How can you say, 'Show us the Father'? Do you not believe that I am in the Father and the Father is in me? The words that I say to you I do not speak on my own authority, but the Father who dwells in me does his works." He concludes in verse 11 by saying, "Believe me when I say that I am in the Father and the Father is in me; or at least believe on the evidence of the works themselves."

1Corinthians 11:3 declares that the head of every woman is man, the head of man is Christ, and the head of Christ is God, meaning that Christ is not the Father or the Holy Spirit, neither is the Father Christ nor the Holy Spirit. If Jesus were the Father, he would have said so when Philip asked him to show them the Father.

The ONENESS of GOD

Instead, he said whoever sees him sees the Father, and that he is in the Father and the Father is in him (they mutually inhabit each other). He is one with the Godhead in essence not in being.

Philip said, "Lord, show us the Father and that will be enough for us." Jesus answered: "Don't you know me, Philip, even after I have been among you such a long time? Anyone who has seen me has seen the Father. How can you say, 'Show us the Father'? Don't you believe that I am in the Father, and that the Father is in me? The words I say to you are not just my own. Rather, it is the Father, living in me, who is doing his work. Believe me when I say that I am in the Father and the Father is in me; or at least believe on the evidence of the miracles themselves.
(Jn. 14:8-12NIV)

God the Father is a spirit being (Jn.4:24) whose presence causes the earth and sky to flee (Rev.20:11). The Bible refers to him as the one on the throne (Rev.5:1 and 7), whose face no one can see and live (Ex.33:20, 1Tim.6:15-16, Jn.1:18, 1Jn.4:12). Scripture declares in Colossians 1:19 that it pleases the Father so well to have all his fullness dwell in Christ so that whoever sees Christ sees the Father. That is why he is the exact representation or the perfect image of the invisible being of God to humankind.

In conclusion, the fullness of God in eternity past consists of his eternal power and divine nature, while his Word, Spirit, and divine essence constitute the fullness of his being in the beginning of his activities. After the incarnation and bodily ascension of his Word to heaven, the Holy Spirit moved from the Father to live in the glorified body of Jesus Christ his Son to bring about the completeness of God's eternal power in bodily form.

FULLNESS OF GOD

Thus, Christ in who dwells bodily, God's Word, Spirit and essence is an extension of God or rather the embodiment of the sum of what makes up his being. For this reason, the Bible declares that in him – i.e. Christ, dwells the fullness of the Godhead bodily (Col.2:9). I like the way the following versions of the Bible put it.

For in Him the entire fullness of God's nature dwells bodily (HCSB). For in Christ lives all the fullness of God in a human body (NLT). For in Him the whole fullness of Deity (the Godhead) continues to dwell in bodily form [giving complete expression of the divine nature] (AMP), For in Christ all the fullness of the Deity lives in bodily form (NIV). For in Christ there is all of God in a human body (TLB), For in him all the fullness of the Godhead dwells bodily (WEB), For in him the whole fulness of deity dwells bodily (RSV)

As earlier explained, the Greek word transliterated (rendered) Godhead or Deity here is "Theotes," and it means the sum of all that makes God who he is. It is the state of being God according to Thayer's definition. The great apostle Paul says in the above passage that it dwells in Christ, the Son of the living God in its entirety.

Since God's Word, Spirit, and divine essence make up his being in eternity past; they all dwell in the glorified body of Jesus of Nazareth, the head of the church. He is the beginning, the firstborn from the dead, that in everything he might have preeminence. Colossians 1:19 says it pleased God to have all his fullness dwell in him – that is, in Christ.

CHAPTER 15

SUMMARY

The Godhead is an invisible eternal self-existent, independent, all-powerful transcendent God from whom all things derived existence (visible or invisible). He is the sole creator and Lord of heaven and earth. We learned in chapter one that he is indivisibly one in essence, and that his being comprises his eternal power and divine nature in eternity.

Chapter two teaches that the very first thing the Godhead did in the order of his works that commenced his activities was to grant his eternal power the right to subsist independently, and it subsisted in him as his Word and Spirit. That is to say, God's work began in eternity when he granted his eternal power, which comes first between the two constituents of his being the right to transition to individual subsistence. This is one of the reasons Bible passage like John1:1 says in the beginning was the Word, the Word was with God and the Word was God, because the Word of God began the beginning and subsisted individually in the Godhead.

The ONENESS of GOD

Chapter three explains that though the Word was by nature one with God, he did not considered the equality he has with the Godhead as something to be used for his advantage. Had he done so, he would not have given up the privileges, rights and dignity of being one with the Godhead in essence to be incarnated. He was conceived and born by the Virgin Mary with half of his DNA derived from the Virgin (a human), and the other copy from the Word of God (Deity), through the operation of the Holy Spirit who made the impossible to happen in the process. He had a complete human and divine nature that perfectly merged in him while on earth, because of his genetic makeup that was composed of both humanity and divinity (he was fully God and human in essence not function, role or title).

Chapter four shows us how the incarnate Word got the name "Jesus of Nazareth, the Son of the living God" and why he offered himself as sin offering on the cross to save humanity from sin and death. It also teaches us how the mortal component in his human nature, which he inherited from the Virgin, was transformed to supernatural (immortality)by the power of the Holy Spirit in order that he might become a life-giving Spirit, after which he ascended bodily to heaven to mediate between the Godhead and humanity.

Chapter five talks about the throne of grace, which is the eternal throne God promised to King David. Jesus of Nazareth, being the long awaited descendant of David sits on the throne and reigns over the house of Jacob forever according to Scripture. It teaches that this throne is the only platform in the courtroom of heaven that a human can boldly approach by faith and prayer, and obtain blessings in Christ.

SUMMARY

Chapter six points out the immense reward that the Godhead gave to Jesus of Nazareth for the ultimate price he paid to rescue humanity from eternal condemnation. It highlights the importance of the reward, and encourages us to keep doing good; given that, God always rewards good works.

Chapter seven talks about the Holy Spirit being God's active power that subsisted in him (the Godhead) as individual being from the beginning like the Word, until the bodily ascension of Jesus of Nazareth, the Son of the living God to the right hand of the Father in the heavenly courtroom. It explains how he (Holy Spirit) emanated from the Godhead to reside in the glorified body of Jesus that he might unite with the Word to bring about the completeness of God's eternal power. The Word and Spirit of God that dwell in Christ constitute the eternal power of God that enables him (the Godhead) to do as he pleases.

Chapter eight teaches that the great white throne is the supreme authority in the courtroom of heaven. It is the seat of the ancient of days, whose presence causes the earth and sky to melt like wax. The throne is reserved for the last and final judgment that shall be administered to the dead, great and small whose names are not written in the Book of Life of the Lamb, and they will be judge according to their deeds as recorded in the books. The sea would give up the dead in it, death and hades would give up the dead that are in them so that all may appear before this throne on the last day. This will happen when Christ hands over the kingdom to God the Father after destroying all dominion, authorities and power.

The ONENESS of GOD

Chapter nine and ten explain why God is the source of all existing things (visible or invisible). The two chapters also highlight the following: (1) the reason the Godhead is both the God, and Father of the Lord Jesus Christ. (2) The basis for Jesus' sonship. (3) Nature of his sonship. (4) How the Word was begotten in eternity past by the Godhead. (5) The significance of divine sonship. (6) Why the sonship of Christian is by adoption. (7) The basis for our sonship in God. (8) Why Jesus' sonship in relation to the Godhead is superior to that of Adam, Israel and Christian. (9) The role of the Holy Spirit, the name and blood of Jesus, the word of God, faith, repentance, and so on in new birth process. (10) How Christians are born again.

Chapter eleven defines the word Elohim and explains how it highlights the plurality of persons in the Godhead. It talks about the nature of God in the beginning of his activities, who God spoke to when he said, "Let us…," and the reason God granted his eternal power the right to subsist in him as individual being, and the concept of interdependence. It also explains why the Godhead is the chief operator and visionary of all divine activities, Jesus the administrator, and the Holy Spirit the sole executor of all divine counsels and purposes.

Chapter twelve explains why the doctrine of the trinity is characterized by a plurality of views, opinions and interpretations. It reveals how the doctrine was developed, why some are confused about it, and why others considered it as heresy or anti-biblical. It also highlights how the doctrine of the trinity is not tritheism, how the word "trinity" should be employed. Lastly, it talks about the difference between God the Father, God the Son and God the Holy Spirit; and God the Father, Jesus the Son of God, and the Holy Spirit.

SUMMARY

Chapter thirteen teaches that the Godhead is by nature one eternal Lord, whose being comprises his eternal power and divine nature. He is the sole creator of all things, which he made for his own pleasure and good will. Due to his love for humanity and the eternal plan that he programmed before time began to be accomplished in Christ, he caused his eternal power to subsist in him as his Word and Spirit. At a specific time, his Word was incarnated, died for the sins of humankind, rose from the dead, ascended bodily to heaven, and sat at the right hand of the Godhead in the courtroom of heaven to represent humanity. He obtained the Holy Spirit from the Father, who also made him Lord and Christ.

It also teaches that though God is one in essence, he exists in three distinct persons as Father, Son and Spirit because of Christ the head of the church. The Father is not the Son or Spirit, the Son is not the Father or the Spirit, and neither is the Spirit the Father nor Son. It stresses that though God exists in three distinct persons as Father, Son and Spirit, he is one in essence.

Chapter fourteen teaches that the fullness of the Godhead, which has to do with the eternal constituents of his being, comprises his eternal power and divine nature in eternity past. The beginning commenced when he caused his eternal power to subsist as his Word and Spirit, which means that the fullness of the Godhead comprises his Word, Spirit and essence in the beginning. After the incarnation, death, resurrection and bodily ascension of his Word to heaven, he obtained the Holy Spirit and formed a unified entity of God's eternal power in the glorified body of Jesus Christ, the head of the church.

The ONENESS of GOD

Christ in whom dwells God's Word, Spirit and essence becomes the embodiment of God's eternal constituent elements.

Furthermore, it emphasizes that Christ is not the Father, Son and Spirit but an extension of the Godhead, and the replicate of all that makes him up. He existed, as the Word in the beginning. He became the Son of God through incarnation and a life-giving Spirit when he rose from death, after which he ascended to heaven and obtained the Holy Spirit from the Father. The Bible declares that it pleased the Father so well to have all his fullness dwell in Christ, so that whoever sees Jesus of Nazareth sees the Father who sent him because he is the exact representation of the Father who none can see and live since his presence causes the heaven and earth to melt like wax.

CHAPTER 16

CONCLUSION

This book unfolds the different phases in the self-revelation of God to humankind. We understand from the written word of God that the whole thing happened because of Christ – the head of the church, and God's love for human race. The subject being a mystery that surpasses human comprehension is centered on the completeness of the Godhead, which consists of the eternal qualities (attributes) that make up his divine being. By the special grace given to the apostle Paul, he writes in his epistle to the Romans, chapter 1 verse 20 that these invisible constituents of the Godhead are his eternal power and divine nature.

For since the creation of the world God's invisible qualities — his eternal power and divine nature — have been clearly seen, being understood from what has been made, so that men are without excuse. (NIV)

God granted his eternal power the right for individual subsistence, and it subsisted in him as his Word (creative power), and his Spirit (active power).

The ONENESS of GOD

When the fixed time came, God sent his Word to save humanity from sin. The Word became flesh, dwelt amongst us, and offered himself as sin offering on the cross to redeem human race from destruction. A price he paid to meet the lawful righteous requirements of the Godhead tagged to the redemption of human souls. Having accomplished his mission on earth, he ascended bodily to heaven and sat at the right hand of God. He obtained the promised Holy Spirit from the Father who also made him Lord and Christ.

Before the incarnation of God's Word, the Godhead existed as God, his Word, and Spirit. However, after his incarnation, and bodily ascension to heaven, the existence of the Godhead changed to "God the Father, Jesus the Son, and the Holy Spirit." Both highlight the fact that though God is one in nature, he exists in three distinct beings. However, this does not signify three separate Gods for that would be tritheism, but one God in three persons (one in essence but distinct in beings).

It is true that many in the body of Christ still hold to the doctrine that the Godhead exists as "God the Father, God the Son and God the Holy Spirit," it is erroneous. There is no place in the Scripture where the Godhead is referred to as God the Father, God the Son, and God the Holy Spirit. Instead, Scripture clearly and repeatedly affirms the existence of the Godhead as God the Father, Jesus the Son of God, and the Holy Spirit.

Second, to affirm that the Godhead exist as God the Father, God the Son, and God the Holy Spirit simply denotes there are three distinct Gods in one person, which implies that we worship three Gods. This affirmation is heresy since it signifies Polytheism (the belief and worship of many gods) and contradicts the following:

CONCLUSION

1. The Holy Scripture, which affirms the oneness of God

2. The nature of God – i.e. indivisibly and inseparably one true eternal God

3. The oneness of the Godhead – i.e. God, his Word and Spirit

The creator and Lord of heaven and earth is one eternal God, who gave his eternal power – being one of the two key constituents of his person the right to subsist individually, and it subsisted as his Word and Spirit. This was before he sent his Word to die for the sins of the world, being incarnated as the Son of God. Subsequently, he raised him from the dead (Acts2:24, 32, 3:15, 26, 4:10, 5:30, 10:40, 13:30, 33, 34, 37, 1Co.6:14, 15:12, 15, 2Co.4:14), and exalted him above the heavens. He sat him at his right hand, crowned him with glory, and made the Holy Spirit to reside in him, in order to unite his Word and Spirit (that makes up his eternal power) in the glorified body of Jesus Christ.

Therefore, to affirm that the Godhead exists as God the Father, God the Son and God the Holy Spirit is a violation of the Holy Scripture, for there is no place in the Bible that confirms it. In the same vein, it is a serious assault against the central truth about the nature of God, which is "Oneness" – that is, the Almighty God is one Lord (Deut.6:4). On the other hand, to affirm that the Father, Son and Spirit are merely different manifestations, roles, titles and functions of God as Modalists claim, rather than individual persons in the Godhead is erroneous.

However, the truth about the nature of God is the tiny line between Tritheism and Modalism.

The ONENESS of GOD

The first stresses threeness in an unbalanced way, and pushes it to a heretical extreme, while the latter stresses oneness in an unbalanced way and pushes it to the opposite heretical extreme. The God of the Bible is intrinsically one in essence and three in persons. That is to say, the Father is not the Son; the Son is not the Holy Spirit, the Holy Spirit is neither the Father nor the Son. The three are individual beings with one nature, purpose and will.

In eternity past, God's eternal power and his divine nature constitute the fullness of his being. The beginning began when he allowed his eternal power to subsist as his Word and Spirit. To be precise, the individual existence of God's Word and Spirit commenced the beginning of God's works. That is why the Scripture declares that in the beginning was the Word (Jn.1:1), and that he is the firstborn over all creation (Col.1:15). Proverb8:22 says he was brought forth as the first of God's works, before his deeds of old, while verse 23 declares he was appointed from eternity and verse 30 adds that he was the craftsman at God's side.

The reason for this is that God begot his creative power in eternity as his Word not as a Son, to be with him by allowing him to subsist as individual being. The subsistence of God's Word and Spirit in the Godhead marked the commencement of God's works. The Word, Spirit and essence of God constitute the fullness of his being in the beginning. After the incarnation, death, resurrection and bodily ascension of God's Word to heaven, he sat at the right hand of the Father and obtained the Holy Spirit from him.

CONCLUSION

The incarnate Word being one in essence with the Godhead came together with the Holy Spirit in the glorified body of Jesus Christ to form a single person. For this reason, Scripture declares that in Christ dwells the fullness of the Godhead bodily because the fundamental constituent of God are his Word, Spirit and essence and they all dwell in Christ in bodily form.

In the end, we have the Godhead as Father over his works, Jesus Christ his Son as Lord, and the Holy Spirit as the sole executor of all divine counsel, which means that the Godhead now exists as "Father, Son and Spirit" (Matt.28:19-20, 1Co.12:4-6, 2Co.13:14, Lk.3:21-22), because of Christ.

Jesus was brought forth in eternity past as the Word of God (Pro.8:22-23, Jn.1:1, Rev.19:13), he became both the Son of God, and the Son of Man through incarnation (Lk.1:31-33, 22:69-70), he died for the sins of humankind, and he was raised for our justification (Rom.4:25). His mortal body (human nature) was clothed with immortality when he rose from the dead and became a life-giving Spirit before ascending bodily to heaven, because flesh and blood cannot inherit the imperishable (1Co.15:45, 50-54, Acts1:9).

He sat at the right hand of the Majesty, called the throne of the Son of God to mediate for human race in the heavenly courtroom (Heb.1:3, 1Tim.2:5). The throne of God on which the Father sits, and the throne of the Lamb on which Christ that embodied God's Word and Spirit sits shall be the supreme authority in the New Jerusalem (Rev.21:22-23, 22:1).

The ONENESS of GOD

In the days of old, God manifested in theophany (Gen.12:7-9, 18:1-33, 32:22-30, Ex.3:2-22), but his inner nature was not disclosed, as it is now reveal in Christ Jesus. The fatherhood of God, sonship of Christ, and the person of the Holy Spirit in the Godhead is the highest order in the self-revelation of the Godhead to humankind.

NOTES

INTRODUCTION

a. Deuteronomy 6:4 (from The Bible Exposition Commentary: Old Testament © 2001-2004 by Warren W. Wiersbe. All rights reserved.)

b. Ibid.

c. DEITY (International Standard Bible Encyclopedia, revised edition, Copyright © 1979 by Wm. B. Eerdmans Publishing Co. All rights reserved)

d. Modalism, Tritheism, or the Pure Revelation of the Triune God, "The Modalistic Concept of the Trinity" by Ron Kangas. Retrieved 12 November 2012 from http://www.contendingforthefaith.org/responses/booklets/modalism.html

e. Bernard, David K., The Oneness of God (Hazelwood, Mo.: Word Aflame Press, 1983), ISBN 0-912315-12-1 pp. 144

f. TRINITY (Nelson's Illustrated Bible Dictionary, Copyright © 1986, Thomas Nelson Publishers)

g. My Views on the Godhead, "Jakes responds to Christianity Today article, Apologetics Journal Criticizes Jakes." Retrieved 14 November 2012 from http://www.christianitytoday.com/ct/2000/februaryweb-only/13.0b.html

h. "T.D. Jakes Embraces Doctrine of the Trinity, Moves Away from 'Oneness' View" by Michael Foust, Baptist Press, found on Christianity today gleanings. Retrieved 7 November 2012, from http://blog.christianitytoday.com/ctliveblog/archives/2012/01/td_jakes_embrac.html

I. "T.D. Jakes says he has embraced doctrine of the Trinity" by Michael Foust, Baptist Press. Retrieved on the 9 November 2012 from http://www.bpnews.net/BPnews.asp?ID=37054

j. Modalism, Tritheism, or the Pure Revelation of the Triune God, "THE TWOFOLDNESS OF DIVINE TRUTH," by Ron Kangas. Retrieved 12 November 2012 from http://www.contendingforthefaith.org/responses/booklets/modalism.html

k. Modalism, Tritheism, or the Pure Revelation of the Triune God, *"AN ATTEMPT TO AVOID THE EXTREMES OF MODALISM AND TRITHEISM"* by Ron Kangas. Retrieved 12 November 2012 from http://www.contendingforthefaith.org/responses/booklets/modalis m.html

Chapter One
NATURE OF GOD

a. Psalms90:2 (from Barnes' Notes, Electronic Database Copyright © 1997, 2003, 2005, 2006 by Biblesoft, Inc. All rights reserved.)

b. Matthew Henry's Commentary on the Whole Bible (Copyright © 1991, Hendrickson Publishers, Inc.) p. 875, ISBN: 978-1-56563-778-8

c. GODHEAD (from International Standard Bible Encyclopaedia, Electronic Database Copyright © 1996, 2003, 2006 by Biblesoft, Inc. All rights reserved)

d. "Spiritual being," *the Free Online Dictionary.* Retrieved 30 November 2012 from http://www.thefreedictionary.com /spiritual+being

e. GOD (from Nelson's Illustrated Bible Dictionary, Copyright © 1986, Thomas Nelson Publishers)

f. NT:1411 (from Thayer's Greek Lexicon, Electronic Database. Copyright © 2000, 2003, 2006 by Biblesoft, Inc. All rights reserved.)

g. DEITY (from International Standard Bible Encyclopedia, revised edition, Copyright © 1979 by Wm. B. Eerdmans Publishing Co. All rights reserved.)

h. Romans 1:20 (from Bible Knowledge Commentary/New Testament Copyright © 1983, 2000 Cook Communications Ministries. All rights reserved.)

I. GOD (from Easton's Bible Dictionary, PC Study Bible formatted electronic database Copyright © 2003, 2006 Biblesoft, Inc. All rights reserved.)

j. TRINITY (from Nelson's Illustrated Bible Dictionary, Copyright © 1986, Thomas Nelson Publishers)

Chapter Two

NATURE OF GOD'S ETERNAL POWER
CREATIVE POWER OF GOD

a. "God, Name of" *Baker's Evangelical Dictionary of Biblical Theology*. Edited by Walter A. Elwell. Retrieved 31 October 2012 from http://www.studylight.org/dic/bed/view.cgi?number=T297

b. The Oneness of God, p. 248

c. Ibid. p. 60

d. "Wisdom," *Oxford dictionaries*. Retrieved 2 December 2012, from http://oxforddictionaries.com/definition/english/wisdom?q=wisdom

e. "Wisdom" Microsoft ®Encarta ® 2009 © 1993-2008 Microsoft Corporation. All rights reserved

f. "Creativity" *Encyclopædia Britannica Online*. Retrieved 28 August 2012, from http://www.britannica.com /Ebchecked/ topic/ 142249/creativity

g. "What Does the Bible Really Teach? ©2005 Watch Tower Bible and Tract Society of Pennsylvania. All Right Reserved. Pp. 41-42

h. Colossians 1:15 (from the Bible Exposition Commentary. Copyright © 1989 by Chariot Victor Publishing, and imprint of Cook Communication Ministries. All rights reserved. Used by permission.)

I. Colossians 1:15 (from Adam Clarke's Commentary, Electronic Database. Copyright © 1996, 2003, 2005, 2006 by Biblesoft, Inc. All rights reserved.)

j. "Firstborn," *the America Heritage Dictionary*. Retrieved 2 January 2013, from http://www.ahdictionary.com/word /search.html?q=firstborn&submit.x=35&submit.y=22

k. John 1:1 (from Adam Clarke's Commentary, Electronic Database. Copyright © 1996, 2003, 2005, 2006 by Biblesoft, Inc. All rights reserved.)

l. John 1:1 (from Bible Knowledge Commentary/New Testament Copyright © 1983, 2000 Cook Communications Ministries. All rights reserved.)

m. John 1:1 (from the UBS New Testament Handbook Series. Copyright © 1961-1997, by United Bible Societies.)

n. John 1:1 (from Vincent's Word Studies in the New Testament, Electronic Database. Copyright © 1997, 2003, 2005, 2006 by Biblesoft, Inc. All rights reserved.)

o. The Oneness of God, p. 140

p. John1:18 (from Bible Knowledge Commentary/New Testament Copyright © 1983, 2000 Cook Communications Ministries. All rights reserved.)

q. John 1:18 (from Jewish New Testament Commentary Copyright © 1992 by David H. Stern. All rights reserved. Used by permission.)

ACTIVE POWER OF GOD

a. The Oneness of God, under the heading *"The Father Is the Holy Ghost."* p. 131

b. Acts 5:3 (from Adam Clarke's Commentary, Electronic Database. Copyright © 1996, 2003, 2005, 2006 by Biblesoft, Inc. All rights reserved.)

c. Acts 5:3-4 (from Jewish New Testament Commentary Copyright © 1992 by David H. Stern. All rights reserved. Used by permission.)

d. Acts 5:4 (from Barnes' Notes, Electronic Database Copyright © 1997, 2003, 2005, 2006 by Biblesoft, Inc. All rights reserved.)

e. GERBER, Michael E. *The E-Myth Revisited*, (HarperCollins, 1995) p. 31

Chapter Three
THE WORD MADE FLESH

a. The oneness of God, p. 221

HOW THE WORD BECAME FLESH

b. Ibid., p.130

c. Dr. Myles Munroe, *The most important person on earth*, (Whitaker house, © 2007 by Dr. Myles Munroe), p. 103

d. Luke 1:34-35 (from the Biblical Illustrator Copyright © 2002, 2003, 2006 Ages Software, Inc. and Biblesoft, Inc.)

FIRST AND SECOND ADAM

e. Hebrews 10:5 (from the Biblical Illustrator Copyright © 2002, 2003, 2006 Ages Software, Inc. and Biblesoft, Inc.)

f. Luke 1:34-35 (from the Biblical Illustrator Copyright © 2002, 2003, 2006 Ages Software, Inc. and Biblesoft, Inc.)

g. Palmer, Ken "Genealogy of Jesus Christ," *Joseph in Christ's genealogy*. Retrieved 27 October 2012, from http://www.lifeofchrist.com/life/genealogy/print.asp

h. Towns, Elmer L. "The Names of Jesus" *CHAPTER SIX, THE BIRTH NAMES OF CHRIST.* pdf

I. "Fertilization," Found on the free online medical dictionary (citing Dorland's Medical Dictionary for Health Consumers © 2007 by Saunders, an imprint of Elsevier, Inc. All rights reserved). Retrieved 31 August 2012, from http://medical-dictionary. thefreedictionary .com/fertilization

j. "What is a chromosome?" *The National Human Genome Research Institute.* Retrieved 21 November 2012, from http://www.genome .gov/26524120#al-1

k. "DNA" *Wikipedia the free encyclopedia.* Retrieved 23 June 2012, from http://en.wikipedia.org/wiki/DNA

l. "Zygote" *Wikipedia the free encyclopedia.* Retrieved 23 June 2012, from http://en.wikipedia.org/wiki/Zygote

m. "Gene," *Found on the free online medical dictionary* (citing Millodot: Dictionary of Optometry and Visual Science, 7th edition © 2009 Butterworth-Heinemann). Retrieved 23 June 2012 from http://medical-dictionary.thefreedictionary.com/gene

n. The Oneness of God, p. 90

o. Dr. Myles Munroe, *The most important person on earth,* (Whitaker house, © 2007 by Dr. Myles Munroe),p. 192

p. The Oneness of God, p. 183

q. Ibid. p. 86

r. Ibid. p. 59

Chapter Four
JESUS OF NAZARETH

a. Jesus (from Easton's Bible Dictionary, PC Study Bible formatted electronic database Copyright © 2003, 2006 Biblesoft, Inc. All rights reserved.)

b. Towns, Elmer L. "The Names of Jesus" *CHAPTER ONE, THE NAME OF JESUS.* Retrieved 25 October 2012, from http: //www.ntslibrary.com/PDF%20Books/The_Names_Of_Jesus%5 BETowns%5D.pdf

c. The Oneness of God, p. 137
d. Ibid. p. 86
e. Ibid. p. 62

Chapter Five
THRONE OF GRACE

a. Genesis 48:18 (from Adam Clarke's Commentary, Electronic Database. Copyright © 1996, 2003, 2005, 2006 by Biblesoft, Inc. All rights reserved.)

Chapter Seven
HOLY SPIRIT

a. The Oneness of God, p. 128
b. Ibid., p. 130
c. Ibid., p. 164
d. Ibid., p. 216
e. Ibid., p. 164
f. The Oneness of God, p. 295

Chapter Nine
FATHERHOOD OF GOD

a. "God, fatherhood of" *Dictionary of Bible Themes*. Retrieved 06 September 2012, from http://www.biblegateway.com/resources dictionary-of-bible-themes/1040-God-fatherhood
b. "God" *Dictionary of Bible Themes*. Retrieved 06 September 2012, from http://www.biblegateway.com/resources/dictionary-of-bible-themes/1015-God
c. The Oneness of God, p. 134
d. Ibid., p. 126
e. Luke 1:35 (from Dake's Annotated Reference Bible Copyright © 1963 by, 1991 Finis Jennings Dake), note d
f. Ibid.
g. Acts 13:33 (from Dake's Annotated Reference Bible), note f.
h. Luke 1:35 (from Adam Clarke's Commentary, Electronic Database. Copyright © 1996, 2003, 2005, 2006 by Biblesoft, Inc. All rights reserved.)

I. The Oneness of God, p. 295

j. Ibid., p. 127

Chapter Ten
DIVINE SONSHIP

a. Acts13:33 (from Dake's Annotated Reference Bible), note f.

b. Webster's Revised Unabridged Dictionary, published 1913 by C. & G. Merriam Co. found on *The Free Dictionary.* Retrieved 16 December 2012 from http://www.thefreedictionary.com/Sonship
NATURE OF THE SONSHIP OF JESUS

c. The oneness of God, p. 122

DIVINE SONSHIP OF JESUS
(Jesus the Son of the living God)

d. Ibid., pp. 121-122

e. Luke 1:35 (from Adam Clarke's Commentary, Electronic Database. Copyright © 1996, 2003, 2005, 2006 by Biblesoft, Inc. All rights reserved.)

f. The Oneness of God, p. 62

HUMAN SONSHIP OF JESUS
(Jesus the Son of Man)

g. Ibid., pp. 302-303

DIVINE SONSHIP OF CHRISTIAN

h. Adoption (from Nelson's Illustrated Bible Dictionary, Copyright © 1986, Thomas Nelson Publishers)

I. Adoption (from International Standard Bible Encyclopaedia, Electronic Database Copyright © 1996, 2003, 2006 by Biblesoft, Inc. All rights reserved.)

j. Brand Chad, Draper Charles, England Archie (General Editors), *Holman Illustrated Bible Dictionary,* "Adoption" © 2003 by Homan Bible Publishers. Nashville, Tennessee. All rights reserved. ISBN 13:978-0-8054-2836-0. p. 29

k. Dr. Alexander, Henry B. *Restoration of the New Testament Church* (Shield of Faith Publication 2007, 2008) p. 38

l. Ibid., pp. 42

m. Ibid., pp. 57

Chapter Eleven
ELOHIM

a. GOD, NAMES OF, *Elohim* (from International Standard Bible Encyclopedia, revised edition, Copyright © 1979 by Wm. B. Eerdmans Publishing Co. All rights reserved.)

b. GOD, NAMES OF, *Elohim* (from Nelson's Illustrated Bible Dictionary, Copyright © 1986, Thomas Nelson Publishers)

c. Elohim, *"God of Israel, with singular verb." from Wikipedia the free encyclopedia.* Retrieved 19 December 2012, from http://en.wikipedia.org/wiki/Elohim#God_of_Israel.2C_with _singular _verb

d̄. The Oneness of God, p. 147

e. GOD (from Smith's Bible Dictionary, PC Study Bible formatted electronic database Copyright © 2003, 2006 by Biblesoft, Inc. All rights reserved.)

f. Covey, Stephen. *The 7Habits of Highly Effective People.* (Free Press, ©1989, 2004) pp. 49, 51

g. The Oneness of God, p. 149

h. Ibid., pp. 151-152

I. Ibid., p. 148

j. GOD, NAMES OF Elohim (from International Standard Bible Encyclopedia, revised edition, Copyright © 1979 by Wm. B. Eerdmans Publishing Co. All rights reserved.)

Chapter Twelve
THE TRINITY

a. Brand Chad, Draper Charles, England Archie (General Editors), *Holman Illustrated Bible Dictionary*, "Trinity" © 2003 by Homan Bible Publishers. Nashville, Tennessee. All rights reserved. ISBN 13:978-0-8054-2836-0. p. 1625

b. Trinity (from Easton's Bible Dictionary, PC Study Bible formatted electronic database Copyright © 2003, 2006 Biblesoft, Inc. All rights reserved.)

c. Trinity (from International Standard Bible Encyclopaedia, Electronic Database Copyright © 1996, 2003, 2006 by Biblesoft, Inc. All rights reserved.)

d. Billy Graham, *The Holy Spirit,* (Word Books Publishers, 1978,) p. 22

e. Dake's Annotated Reference Bible, p. 280

f. Trinity (from International Standard Bible Encyclopaedia, Electronic Database Copyright © 1996, 2003, 2006 by Biblesoft, Inc. All rights reserved.)

g. Dake's Annotated Reference Bible, p. 280

h. Trinity (from International Standard Bible Encyclopaedia, Electronic Database Copyright © 1996, 2003, 2006 by Biblesoft, Inc. All rights reserved.)

I. Holman Illustrated Bible Dictionary, p. 1625

j. Matthew 28:19 (from Jewish New Testament Commentary Copyright © 1992 by David H. Stern. All rights reserved. Used by permission.)

k. Holman Illustrated Bible Dictionary, p. 1625

l. The Oneness of God, p. 294-295

m. "Jakes responds to Christianity Today article, Apologetics Journal Criticizes Jakes" *My Views on the Godhead*. Retrieved 14 November 2012 from http://www.christianitytoday.com /ct /2000/ februaryweb-only/13.0b.html

n. TRINITY (from International Standard Bible Encyclopaedia, Electronic Database Copyright © 1996, 2003, 2006 by Biblesoft, Inc. All rights reserved.)

o. Ibid.

Chapter Thirteen
ONENESS OF GOD

a. Dr. Alexander, Henry B. *Restoration of the New Testament Church* (Shield of Faith Publication 2007, 2008) p. 30

b. Ibid., pp. 126 – 27

c. Ibid., p. 131

Chapter Fourteen
FULLNESS OF GOD

a. The Oneness of God, p. 216

OTHER REFERENCES

1. MATTHEW HENRY'S COMMENTARY ON THE WHOLE BIBLE Complete and Unabridged in One Volume Copyright © 1991 by Hendrickson Publishers, Inc. ISBN: 978-1-56563-778-8

2. THE NEW STRONG'S EXPANDED EXHAUSTIVE CONCORDANCE OF THE BIBLE, Red-Letter ed. © 2001 by Thomas Nelson Publishers ISBN 13: 978-0-7852-4539-1

3. Robert P. Lightner, *The God of the Bible, An Introduction to the Doctrine of God,* Baker Book House, Grand Rapids, 1973

4. Lewis Sperry Chafer Systematic Theology, Vol. 1, Abridged Edition, John F. Walvoord, Editor, Donald K. Campbell, Roy B. Zuck, Consulting Editors, Victor Books, Wheaton, IL, 1988.

5. Louis Berkhof, *Systematic Theology*, Banner of Truth, London, 1968

6. *The Theological Dictionary of the New Testament, Abridged in One Volume*, Gerhard Kittel and Gerhard Friedrich, editors, Eerdmans, Grand Rapids, 1985, electronic media

7. Kenneth Boa, *Unraveling the Big Questions About God*, Zondervan, Grand Rapids, 1988

8. Francis Schaeffer, *The God Who is There*, InterVarsity Press, Downers Grove, IL, 1968

IMPORTANT
ABBREVIATIONS

Gen..Genesis
Ex. ....Exodus
Lev. .... Leviticus
Num. ....Numbers
Deut. ....Deuteronomy
Josh. ....J oshua
Judg. ....Judges
1Sa. 1Samuel
2Sa. 2Samuel
1Ki. 1Kings
2Ki. ....2 Kings
1Ch. 1Chronicles
2Ch. 2Chronicles
Neh. ....Nehemiah
Esth. ....Esther
Ps. .... Psalms
Pr. ....Proverbs
Ecc. ....Ecclesiastics
SoS... Song of Songs
Is. ....Isaiah
Jer..Jeremiah
Lam. ....Lamentations
Ezek. ....Ezekiel
Dan. ....Daniel
Hos. ....Hosea
Jon. ....Jonah
Mic. ....Micah
Nah. ....Nahum
Hab. .... Habakkuk
Zeph. .... Zephaniah
Hag. .... Haggai
Zec... Zechariah

Matt. ....Matthew
Mk. ....Mark
Lk. ....Luke
Jn. .... John
Rom. .... Romans
1Co. 1Corinthians
2Co. 2Corinthians
Gal. .... Galatians
Eph. ....Ephesians
Phi. ....Philippians
Col. .... Colossians
1Thes. 1Thessalonians
2Thes. 2Thessalonians
1Tim. 1Timothy
2Tim. 2Timothy
Heb. .... Hebrews
Jas. ....James
1Pet. 1Peter
2Pet. 2Peter
1Jn. 1John
2Jn. 2John
3Jn. 3John
Rev. ....Revelation

PRAYER OF SALVATION

The gospel message also known as the word of faith, belief and open confession play distinct roles in the salvation process, according to Romans10:8-10. The word of faith produces the faith we need to please God and be at peace with him (Heb.11:6), believing that God raised Jesus from death causes him to impute his righteousness that is by faith to us (Rom.4:22-25). Confessing the lordship of Jesus makes God to infuse our spirit with his eternal life for rebirth.

Salvation does not come by merely verbalizing the *Sinner's Prayer* without faith in Christ atoning sacrifice that comes from hearing the gospel message, repentance from dead works, and open confession of Jesus Christ as lord and savior.

1. Believe in your heart that Christ is the Son of the living God
2. Believe he died on the cross for your sins and iniquities
3. Believe that God raised him from the dead after three days for your justification
4. Believe he is at the right hand of the Father in heaven interceding for you
5. Believe that only Christ has the legitimate right to give eternal life to humans
6. Ask him to forgive your sins and wash you by his blood
7. Openly declare him lord of your life from the depth of your heart
8. Invite him to come and dwell in you
9. Ask him to write your name in the book of life

And this is the testimony: God has given us eternal life, and this life is in his Son. He who has the Son has life; he who does not have the Son of God does not have life. I write these things to you who believe in the name of the Son of God so that you may know that you have eternal life.
(1 Jn. 5:11-14 NIV)

If you confess with your mouth the Lord Jesus and believe in your heart that God has raised Him from the dead, you will be saved. For with the heart one believes unto righteousness, and with the mouth confession is made unto salvation.
(Rom. 10:9-10 NKJV)

Salvation is found in no one else, for there is no other name under heaven given to men by which we must be saved.
(Acts 4:12 NIV)

If we confess our sins, He is faithful and righteous to forgive us our sins and to cleanse us from all unrighteousness.
(1 Jn. 1:9-10 HCSB)

Once you finish reading the above portion of scriptures, you can make the following confession with me from the depth of your heart. Believe it as you speak, and you shall be saved in Jesus name.

Dear Jesus,

I believe that you died on the cross for my sins, and rose on the third day for my justification. You took away my sins, iniquities, infirmities and blotted out the handwriting of ordinances that were against me by your blood. You were bruised for my transgressions, and became a curse for me in order to redeem my soul from death.

I beseech you Lord to come into my life today, and make my heart your dwelling place. I confess you now as my Lord and Savior. Write my name in the book of life, and make me a new person. Thank you Lord Jesus for saving me. Amen

Congratulation!

Since what may be known about God is plain to them, because God has made it plain to them. For since the creation of the world God's invisible qualities — his eternal power and divine nature — have been clearly seen, being understood from what has been made, so that men are without excuse. For although they knew God, they neither glorified him as God nor gave thanks to him, but their thinking became futile and their foolish hearts were darkened. Although they claimed to be wise, they became fools and exchanged the glory of the immortal God for images made to look like mortal man and birds and animals and reptiles.

(Rom. 1:19-23 NIV)

Follow me on **f** Caesar Benedo

Email.caesben11@yahoo.com

Dépot Légal N° 8113 du 09 / 09 / 2015

Bibliothèque National, 3ème Trimestre